BLAMELESS

Learning to walk in the freedom of Christ without being overcome by the guiltiness of the culture.

DYLAN M. RUTLAND

©2025 by Dylan Rutland

Uncaused Publishing
Orlando, FL

Printed in the United States of America

All rights reserved. No part of this publication may be reproduced, stored in a retrieval system, or transmitted in any form or by any means-for example, electronic, photocopy, recording-without the prior written permission of the publisher. The only exception is brief quotations in printed reviews.

Rutland, Dylan
Blameless: Learning to walk in the freedom of Christ without being overcome by the guiltiness of the culture.

ISBN: 979-8-9898982-4-4

To the seeker, the struggler, the saint—
may you stand firm and walk upright.

When you the weight is heavy and path unclear,
may His Word be your light.

When doubt whispers and fear grip you,
may his truth be your steady ground.

When you fall, may grace lift you up,
for in Him, the blameless are found.

ACKNOWLEDGEMENTS

No book is ever written alone. While the words on these pages may have come from my heart, they were shaped by the people God placed in my life—those who have encouraged, challenged, and walked alongside me on this journey.

First, I give thanks to the Lord Jesus Christ. Without Him, I would have nothing—no purpose, no hope, no redemption. Every word in this book exists because of His grace and mercy. He is the One who reached for me when I was lost, and the One who makes me blameless, and the One who continues to shape me in ways I cannot fully comprehend. Every struggle, every season of wandering, every failure—He has turned it all for good. His voice called me back time and time again, and His love has never wavered, even when mine did.

There is no amount of gratitude that could ever match the depth of what He has done for me. The words of this book, my life, my future—it all belongs to Him. My greatest desire is that every page would reflect His heart, that every word would point back to Him, and that even one person might be drawn closer to His presence because of it.

To the One who never gave up on me—to the God who sees, who restores, and who calls us by name—I give all glory, all honor, and all praise.

To my wife, Alayna—you are the most tangible evidence of God's mercy in my life. Through every season, every challenge, every late-night conversation, and every unspoken prayer, you have been my constant. Your love is fierce, your faith unwavering, and your presence in my life is a gift I could never deserve. You have seen me at my lowest and still believed in the man God was shaping me to be. Thank you for your patience, your encouragement, and for always pointing me back to Jesus. I love you!

To my boys, Liam and Levi—my greatest joys, and my living reminders of God's faithfulness.

Liam, my firstborn, my little traveler, you've been by my side through so many adventures. You have sat in church pews across the country, listening to sermons in places you'll barely remember, and carried the excitement of every city and every long road trip with a joy that only a child can. From snow-capped mountains, to vast rolling hills, to wide open fields of corn and sugar cane, to little rain puddles on overcast days, you have taught me more about wonder, about curiosity, and about seeing the world through fresh eyes.

Watching you grow has been one of the greatest blessings of my life. I pray that wherever life takes you, you will always follow the voice of God with the same excitement and trust you've had on every journey with us.

Levi, my miracle boy, you were born after two heartbreaks, after two moments when we thought we might never meet you. But God had a plan, and in His perfect timing, He gave us you. You are proof that His promises never fail, that His goodness is not limited by our fears, and that He always writes a better story than we could imagine. Every time I look at you, I am reminded of the prayer we prayed and the faithfulness of the God who answered them. You are a gift, and my prayer for you is that always know how deeply loved and wanted you are—not just by us, but by the God who created you with purpose.

My boys, you will always be my greatest ministry, my most important calling. If I accomplish nothing else in this life but to lead you to Jesus,

I will have done well. Remember, many are called, few are chosen, but you are chosen of the Lord. I love you more than words can say.

To my pastor and mentors—you have shaped my life in ways I can never express. Pastor Joseph Adams, your leadership and wisdom have given me direction when I felt lost. You have spoken truth into my life, sometimes with encouragement, other times with correction, but always with love. To the men who have poured into me—whether through preaching, personal conversations, or simple acts of faithfulness—you have left a mark on my life that will never fade. Your examples of integrity and devotion have helped mold me into the

man I am becoming. To my church family—your prayers, encouragement, and faithfulness have been a source of strength. I am blessed to be surrounded by people who truly love God and one another.

To my friends and fellow ministers—than you for the conversations, the excited discussions, and the moments that sharpened my understanding of faith, the Word, and life. Your friendship has been invaluable.

And finally, to you, the reader—thank you for taking this journey with me. My prayer is that as you walk through these pages, God speaks to you in a way that only He can.

With gratitude,
Dylan Rutland

CONTENTS

Introduction 11

1. The Path to Blamelessness 15
2. It Is Well 23
3. Sweet Hour of Prayer 39
4. Give Thanks, In This? 47
5. Let Go and Let God 65
6. Embrace The Word 81
7. Prove It! 93
8. Cling to the Good 115
9. Abstain From All Appearance of Evil 133

Conclusion 153

INTRODUCTION

Blameless. At first glance, the word can be intimidating. What does it truly mean to be blameless, and how crucial is it to achieve? The reality is, we cannot enter heaven unless we are blameless. That is a daunting thought, as heaven allows no sin, no unrighteousness, and no ungodliness. "For all have sinned and fall short of the glory of God" (Romans 3:23). So, how do we become blameless? If we are honest with ourselves, we have already fallen short. When we reflect on this, it's natural to ask, "What can I do now? I am already guilty of transgressing against the Lord."

In this exploration, I will delve into the scriptures to uncover how we can be preserved blameless until the coming of our Lord Jesus Christ. "If we confess our sins, He is faithful and just to forgive us our sins and to cleanse us from all unrighteousness" (1 John 1:9). This scripture provides hope, but how do we actively live this out? How do we walk in the way of blamelessness, knowing we've already sinned and fallen short?

The Apostle Paul speaks directly to this in his letter to Timothy. He reminds the church—and us today—that every word of God is inspired and useful "for doctrine, for reproof, for correction, for instruction in righteousness" (2 Timothy 3:16). Paul's message to the Thessalonians is not just a passing suggestion. He charges the recipients of this epistle with a solemn responsibility. "I charge you by the Lord that this epistle be read unto all the holy brethren," he writes in 1 Thessalonians 5:27. This is no casual statement. In some of his other writings, Paul distinguishes between his personal opinion and divine commandment, but here, he is delivering God's message, directly inspired by the Holy Spirit, with clear instructions on how we must live and serve God.

Paul's call is for us to be sanctified wholly, with God's plan being for our entire spirit, soul, and body to be preserved blameless until the coming of our Lord Jesus Christ. "May the God of peace Himself sanctify you completely; and may your whole spirit, soul, and body be preserved blameless at the coming of our Lord Jesus Christ" (1 Thessalonians 5:23). This is the ultimate goal of every believer—to be sanctified wholly, to be kept blameless until the return of our Savior.

We have to be blameless. We must be blameless. Adam and Eve were cast out of the Garden of Eden because they lost their blamelessness. Since that day, humanity has been blameworthy. The innocence we were created to live in was lost, and we became people worthy of blame. We were driven out of God's covenant, and instead entered into a covenant with death. And that is where blame leaves us—in the clutches of death. "For the wages of sin is death, but the gift of God is eternal life in Christ Jesus our Lord" (Romans 6:23). Blamelessness, however, leads us to life—eternal life.

But if we are worthy of blame, what hope do we have of becoming blameless? It's essential to acknowledge the seriousness of our fallen nature. We have already fallen short of God's glory. We have sinned. We have missed our chance. The gravity of this situation is often misunderstood, which is why I state it bluntly: there is no room for softening this truth. We have already missed our chance to enter heaven on our own. That ship has sailed. Our only hope of heaven is through Jesus Christ. "Jesus said to him, 'I am the way, the truth, and the life. No one comes to the Father except through Me'" (John 14:6).

So, how does blamelessness happen for someone like me? Someone who has sinned, who has transgressed against God's law, and broken His covenant? How can I stand blameless before the Lord on the day of judgment? It happens through the Gospel of Jesus Christ. His death on the cross, His atonement for our sins, His resurrection—it is through these that we are given the opportunity to be made blameless. "For God so loved the world that He gave His only begotten Son, that whoever believes in Him should not perish but have everlasting life" (John 3:16).

Blamelessness is not something we can achieve on our own. It is the result of God's grace working in us through the sacrifice of Jesus Christ. As Philippians 1:6 says, "Being confident of this very thing, that He who has begun a good work in you will complete it until the day of Jesus Christ." God is the one who works in us, sanctifying us, preserving us, and ultimately making us blameless before Him.

Paul, in his first letter to the Thessalonians, encourages us to pursue blamelessness not only through faith in Christ but also by actively walking in the Spirit. "May the Lord make your love increase and overflow for each other and for everyone else, just as ours does for you. May He strengthen your hearts so that you will be blameless and holy in the presence of our God and Father when our Lord Jesus comes with all His holy ones" (1 Thessalonians 3:12-13). This pursuit is not passive—it requires an active, ongoing submission to God's will.

This journey toward blamelessness requires a response. We cannot stand still. As you walk through these pages, my prayer is that you will seek God with your whole heart. Open yourself to His transforming power. Know that He has already provided the way to blamelessness through Jesus Christ—but it is up to us to walk that path daily, in faith and in obedience.

We must embrace this truth: we are made blameless through the blood of Christ, through His sacrifice, and through the sanctifying work of the Holy Spirit. The Apostle Paul's words are a clear charge to each of us to live blamelessly, and to live with purpose, knowing that Jesus is coming again.

As you read this book, I urge you to let these truths shape your heart. The call to blamelessness is not a burden—it is an invitation to life. Through Christ, we can stand blameless before God, not because of our own efforts, but because of His perfect sacrifice.

CHAPTER 1

THE PATH TO BLAMELESSNESS

WHERE THE PATH BEGINS

Ephesians 2:8-9 states, "For by grace are ye saved through faith; and that not of yourselves: it is the gift of God: Not of works, lest any man should boast." It is indeed the gift of God, a profound and unearned favor given to us through Christ.

On the Day of Pentecost, recorded in Acts 2, the Spirit of God was poured out upon the believers, fulfilling the prophecy of Joel that God would pour out His Spirit on all flesh. This event marked the birth of the Christian church and empowered the disciples to preach the gospel with boldness. Those who witnessed this miraculous event were deeply concerned for their souls. They saw something extraordinary happening—the Holy Spirit had come with fire, and their hearts were stirred.

The crowd, moved by conviction, asked Peter and the apostles, "Men and brethren, what shall we do?" Peter's response was clear and powerful, delivering exactly what Jesus had instructed before His ascension into heaven. It was a message that would go on to change the world, turning cities upside down wherever it was preached. Peter preached Jesus and provided them with the instructions for salvation, speaking with the boldness that only the Holy Spirit can provide.

Acts 2:38-39 says, "Then Peter said unto them, Repent, and be baptized every one of you in the name of Jesus Christ for the remission of sins, and ye shall receive the gift of the Holy Ghost. 39. For the promise is unto you, and to your children, and to all that are afar off, even as many as the Lord our God shall call." This simple message—the death, burial, and resurrection of Jesus Christ, with the invitation to repent, be baptized, and receive the Holy Ghost—continues to bring salvation to souls around the world.

This salvation must be received, not earned. Those sins must be remitted, blotted out, washed away, and covered by the blood of Jesus Christ, or we cannot enter or even see the Kingdom of God. This is where the path of the journey to blamelessness begins: in the saving work of Christ and in our response to His call.

WALKING IN BLAMELESSNESS

In John 3:3-8, Jesus explained the necessity of being born again. "Except a man be born again, he cannot see the kingdom of God… except a man be born of water and of the Spirit, he cannot enter into the kingdom of God." This transformation begins with baptism and the infilling of the Holy Spirit. Without the blamelessness of Jesus Christ, we still carry the weight of our blame. But in Christ, our sins are washed away.

When I was baptized in the name of Jesus Christ, I believed fully that His blood paid the price for my sins. His death on the cross was sufficient to vanquish the sins of humanity, destroy death, and give me access to eternal life. I repented, turning away from my sins, and when I was buried in the waters of baptism, my old self was left behind in that watery grave. I rose up with a new identity, covered by the name of Jesus Christ. No longer was I "Wretched Dylan," but now I am seen as a blameless son of God.

It is a profound mystery and a glorious truth that when we put on Christ, we are no longer viewed by God through the lens of our failures but through the righteousness of His Son. This is how we are blameless—not because of anything we have done, but because of everything He has done.

GOD'S INCREDIBLE EXCHANGE

The old hymn "Amazing Grace," written by John Newton, declares, "Amazing grace, how sweet the sound that saved a wretch like me." When we consider that we deserve not just the grave, but hell itself, it is truly by God's grace that we have access to His promises. Chief among these promises is the gift of sanctification by His Spirit and reconciliation to Himself.

God offers us an incredible exchange: "Give me all that you did wrong, and I'll take your punishment on the cross. I'll give you all that I did right, and you can receive my reward and glory." What kind of deal is that? That, my friend, is amazing grace. This is where we find our blamelessness. It's not that we have never done anything wrong—it's that we are putting all of our hope in Jesus Christ. His righteousness is our blamelessness. There is no blame in Him, and by standing in Him, we can now stand blameless.

Imagine that: in Jesus, we are no longer seen as guilty sinners. Instead, we are covered by the One who was blameless. It's a reality that goes beyond comprehension. It's grace upon grace, and it's this grace that sustains us in our walk.

ABSTAINING FROM ALL APPEARANCE OF EVIL

Paul's epistle to the Thessalonians provides us with this crucial instruction: "Abstain from all appearance of evil" (1 Thessalonians 5:22). This statement is profound, yet it can feel impossible. How can we, in a world so full of corruption, even begin to abstain from the appearance of evil, let alone evil itself?

When I first read this verse, I remember feeling a deep sense of inadequacy. Evil surrounds us at every turn—on our phones, in the workplace, in our relationships. The world is saturated with temptations, and as much as we might try, our strength alone is never enough to resist it all. But notice the wisdom in Paul's words: it's not just about avoiding evil acts, but even the appearance of evil.

This call is a higher standard than most of us would set for ourselves. But it's also an invitation to walk in God's holiness, not in our own strength but by His Spirit. When we abstain from the appearance of evil, we avoid the places where our weaknesses can be exposed. We don't just fight the enemy head-on; we build walls around our hearts and minds that prevent temptation from even getting close.

Evil, in its many forms, seeks to enter our lives in subtle ways. It creeps in through distractions, compromises, and half-truths. And yet, with the power of the Holy Spirit, we are called to stand guard against even the slightest appearance of it.

THE ADVERSARY'S SNARES

2 Peter 2:22 says, "But it is happened unto them according to the true proverb, The dog is turned to his own vomit again; and the sow that was washed to her wallowing in the mire." This paints a vivid picture of those who have been cleansed but return to their sinful ways, ensnared once again by the enemy. The Bible calls this "backsliding," and it's a real danger for every believer. We often recognize when we are weak in our faith because we start revisiting the places, habits, and mindsets that God originally delivered us from.

Paul teaches that it's not just about becoming blameless; it's about being preserved blameless until the coming of our Lord Jesus Christ. The goal is not merely a momentary victory over sin but a sustained, Spirit-filled walk that keeps us in God's grace. Paul didn't simply say, "Abstain from evil and call it a day." Instead, he laid a solid foundation for every born-again believer—a foundation that enables us to be preserved blameless, to walk uprightly, and to abstain from all appearance of evil.

If we can gain victory over the appearance of evil, the acts of sin will not even have a chance to take root. By abstaining, we avoid the fierceness of God's anger and remain in His peace.

THE ROLE OF THE HOLY SPIRIT

We must submit ourselves to God's word and His Spirit. Often, we are tempted to embrace only the parts of His word that suit our preferences, but this is dangerous. There are many who seek out teachers to suit their "itching ears" (2 Timothy 4:3). In reality, both the teacher and the listener have itching ears, each looking for validation rather than correction. They want praise for where they are and what they do, avoiding any word that challenges or rebukes them.

But the truth is, we cannot walk blamelessly by our own strength. We cannot walk blamelessly by avoiding the truth that confronts our habits, thought patterns, and cycles of living. If we try to abstain from all appearance of evil without acknowledging the power of the Holy Spirit, we will fail. It is by the Spirit of God that we overcome evil, for the flesh is weak and incapable of victory on its own. The Spirit of God within you is the earnest of your inheritance. It is the down payment of your salvation, the guarantee of your blamelessness before God.

PREPARING FOR PRESERVATION

1 Thessalonians 5:16-21 states, "Rejoice evermore. 17. Pray without ceasing. 18. In every thing give thanks: for this is the will of God in Christ Jesus concerning you. 19. Quench not the Spirit. 20. Despise not prophesyings. 21. Prove all things; hold fast that which is good."

In these verses, Paul lays out the foundation for how we are to live blamelessly. Rejoice evermore—our hearts must be filled with joy in the Lord. Pray without ceasing—a life saturated with prayer is essential. In everything give thanks—gratitude aligns our hearts with God's will. Quench not the Spirit—we must be sensitive to the leading of the Holy Spirit. Despise not prophesyings—we are to be open to God's voice through His messengers. Prove all things—test everything against the truth of God's word. Hold fast that which is good—cling to what is pure, holy, and righteous.

This is how we prepare ourselves to be preserved blameless. This is how we live in the Spirit, walking in God's truth and abstaining from all appearance of evil. It is a daily choice, a moment-by-moment reliance on God's grace and the guidance of His Spirit.

WALKING IN THE SPIRIT

So, how do we begin? First, we must be honest with ourselves. Are there areas in our lives where the appearance of evil has crept in? Have we relied on our own strength rather than walking in the Spirit? Now is the time to recommit ourselves to the path of blamelessness, trusting not in our ability but in the power of God's Spirit.

I challenge you to take a moment to reflect. Where are the snares? Where are the pitfalls? God has provided a way out. "No temptation has overtaken you except what is common to mankind. And God is faithful; He will not let you be tempted beyond what you can bear. But when you are tempted, He will also provide a way out so that you can endure it" (1 Corinthians 10:13).

Let us walk in this truth, trusting that He who began a good work in us will complete it. Let us pursue blamelessness, not by our strength but by His Spirit. And when we stand before Him, we will hear those blessed words: "Well done, good and faithful servant."

CHAPTER 2

IT IS WELL

THE CALL TO REJOICE

The first thing Paul instructs the people of God to do in order to abstain from the appearance of evil is: "Rejoice evermore." This command is found in 1 Thessalonians 5:16 and is at the forefront of these concise instructions, serving as the foundation. If you are trying to abstain from all appearance of evil but are not rejoicing evermore, you are far more likely to fall into temptation. The first thing God wants us to do is rejoice.

The Bible takes rejoicing very seriously. In fact, the Apostle Paul writes to the church at Philippi, "Rejoice in the Lord always..." Now, rejoicing from time to time is understandable, but rejoicing always? That requires real commitment. Paul didn't stop there, though; it's as if he is saying, "In case you didn't grasp the urgency of this command the first time, I am going to say it again. Rejoice in the Lord always: and again I say, Rejoice."

REJOICING BEYOND EMOTION

To rejoice in the Lord is not merely an emotional reaction. While there is emotion involved, and emotion can arise from rejoicing, it goes much deeper. When we think of rejoicing, we often picture making a joyful noise unto the Lord—shouting, lifting our voices in praise, coming into His presence with singing. All of that is good; all of that is great. Praise is what we do as God's holy nation and peculiar people. There is no denying that praise is fitting for the upright. It is a beautiful thing. However, rejoicing is more profound than the words of praise that come from our mouths and are directed toward God.

I am not talking about emotion alone. I am talking about something that is harnessed praise. Rejoicing is harnessed worship. The reality is that our emotions can take us to places we never thought we would go. Our emotions can shift, and in an instant, our attitude changes. When our attitude changes, so does our countenance. Our spirit can become depressed because of how powerful our emotions are within us.

Rejoicing can certainly be fueled by emotions, but it is not dependent on them. Rejoicing is consistent, regardless of our emotions in the moment. It is steady, no matter what we are going through. In fact, rejoicing means "to be glad, to be calmly happy, to be well off." Rejoicing means "to be well."

UNDERSTANDING REJOICING

Before we can truly abstain from all appearance of evil, we need to understand and receive the revelation of what it means to rejoice. We must be glad; we must be well; we must be well-off. Now, this might make us think of certain individuals in our family or society about whom we say, "They are well-off." But that's not the point here.

Look at 2 Kings 4:25-26, So she went and came unto the man of God to Mount Carmel. And it came to pass, when the man of God saw her afar off, that he said to his servant, Behold, yonder is that Shunammite: 26. Run now, I pray thee, to meet her, and say unto her, Is it well with thee? Is it well with thy husband? Is it well with the child? And she answered, It is well."

"I am well"—regardless of what is happening around me. I am calmly happy despite the storm that has erupted in my world. I am rejoicing not just today, not just tomorrow, but evermore. Rejoicing requires restraint. It requires the fruit of the Spirit known as self-control. It is the control of oneself, but not in the flesh. It is a miracle of God, accomplished by His Spirit and His Word.

REJOICING IN EVERY DAY

Psalm 118:24 says, "This is the day which the Lord hath made; we will rejoice and be glad in it." What day? This day. Whatever calendar day you find yourself in right now—this day. What day was the psalmist referring to in his writing? This day. If I sound redundant, it is on purpose. Ask me again tomorrow, and I will say the same thing: this day. Ask me on any day of the week, and my answer will still be the same. Regardless of what is happening in our lives, this is still the day that the Lord has made, so let us rejoice in it. Let us be well. Let us be calmly happy. Let us be glad in it.

Now, I know this might seem like an impossible picture. We start thinking, "I have faith, but come on. There are just some days when I am not glad. I am not well. I am not calm, and I am certainly not happy about it." I understand that, and so does the Lord. But we must remember that all goodness comes from Him.

I am convinced that the ability to rejoice evermore, to rejoice with those who rejoice, and to rejoice in the Lord always is directly tied to, and a result of, the fruit of the Spirit called joy being evident in our lives. Our flesh cannot produce the kind of joy we are talking about here. As I mentioned earlier, these are miracles that God performs.

Do not ever wonder if you believe in miracles. You do believe in miracles. It is a miracle that you are sane right now. It is a miracle that you are well right now. It is a miracle that you are happy right now. Know that, believe that, and understand that it is a miracle of the Spirit, not a work of the flesh, for you to be able to rejoice.

THE ORIGIN OF REJOICING

So, if our flesh cannot produce this kind of rejoicing, then where does it come from? How do we rejoice evermore? How do we reach the point in our lives where we can truly say, "I am rejoicing in the Lord"? In the Bible, if you truly want to understand something, you need to go back to where it was first mentioned. The first instance of rejoicing is found in Exodus 18. It is crucial that we grasp this concept in our hearts because we cannot abstain from all appearance of evil if we do not have the proper foundation built within our spirit.

Exodus 18:5-11, "And Jethro, Moses' father-in-law, came with his sons and his wife unto Moses into the wilderness, where he encamped at the mount of God: 6. And he said unto Moses, I thy father-in-law Jethro am come unto thee, and thy wife, and her two sons with her. 7. And Moses went out to meet his father-in-law, and did obeisance, and kissed him; and they asked each other of their welfare; and they came into the tent. 8. And Moses told his father-in-law all that the Lord had done unto Pharaoh and to the Egyptians for Israel's sake, and all the travail that had come upon them by the way, and how the Lord delivered them. 9. And Jethro rejoiced for all the goodness which the LORD had done to Israel, whom he had delivered out of the hand of the Egyptians. 10. And Jethro said, Blessed be the LORD, who hath delivered you out of the hand of the Egyptians, and out of the hand of Pharaoh, who hath delivered the people from under the hand of the Egyptians. 11. Now I know that the LORD is greater than all gods: for in the thing wherein they dealt proudly he was above them."

As Moses spoke to his father-in-law about all that Israel had endured—how Pharaoh had oppressed them, and how the Lord had brought them out of bondage and rescued them from Pharaoh—Jethro began to rejoice. Now, Jethro was not a prophet, and he certainly wasn't the "Beverly Hillbillies" Jethro either. He was simply trying to understand everything Moses was telling him. The more Moses shared, the more Jethro realized that God had done something truly extraordinary. At the report of Moses, Jethro rejoiced. He was not a Hebrew by blood or birth, but something stirred in Jethro's spirit, and he began to rejoice.

GOD IS IN CONTROL

The plagues that the Lord brought upon the Egyptians directly confronted the Egyptian deities. If you were on Israel's side, they were the wonders of the Lord. But if you were in Egypt, they were the plagues of the Israelite God. With each plague, the Egyptian gods were exposed as false and powerless, and as a result, the Lord was magnified and glorified.

Now, let's get this picture clear. Jethro is Moses' father-in-law. Moses is on what might seem like a harebrained quest to deliver the children of Israel out of Egypt. During this time, Jethro has been taking care of his daughter and grandchildren while Moses is out in the wilderness, smiting rocks and performing miracles. Naturally, I can imagine Jethro feeling a bit nervous about all of this. If he was like any good father, he was probably wondering, "Is this really the right guy for my daughter?"

So, Jethro comes down to meet Moses, perhaps a bit apprehensively, to see how things are going. When Moses gives a good report of all that God did for Israel in Egypt, something changes. As Moses shares these stories of God's wonders, Jethro rejoices. In that moment, a happy calm washes over him. He realizes that God is truly in control, and his heart can rest in that knowledge.

I don't know what everyone is facing at this moment in their life, but I do know this: God is in control. Be well. Be glad. Let the peaceful calm of the Holy Ghost settle upon your soul right now, in Jesus' name. Rejoice evermore.

We have all experienced times of chaos and confusion—when the storms of life are crashing down around us, lightning is flashing, thunder is roaring, and it feels like everything is falling apart. It's that kind of spiritual and mental fog where you can't tell which way is up or down, and you're just doing your best to hold on with what little you have left. Then, all of a sudden, there comes a moment of clarity: you realize that you need to keep holding on to God's unchanging hand. In that moment, a calm settles over your spirit as you remember that God is still in control. That is rejoicing. Rest in that revelation. Lay your head on your pillow at night and find peace in the security of God's power. Be glad. Be well. Be calmly happy.

LEARNING TO REJOICE

"How is everything going?" the prophet asked the Shunammite woman in 2 Kings 4. Now, do you think her response was, "Do you really want to know the answer to that question?" Thank God, it's just a formality when someone asks, "How are you doing?" Most of the time, we don't answer that question as honestly as we could. We usually reply with, "I'm fine. Doing well, thank you. How are you?"

Is that how the Shunammite woman answered the prophet? Did she say, "Do you really want to know? My son just died. The child you prophesied into this world is lying dead in your chamber right now. You really want to know what's going on in my life? There. Are you happy?" No, she did not respond that way. Instead, she said, "It is well." She rejoiced. She declared, "It is well."

REJOICING AMIDST FEAR

This is the kind of rejoicing Jesus referred to when He said in John 8:56, "Your father Abraham rejoiced to see my day: and he saw it, and was glad." The entire way up that mountain, with his promised son Isaac by his side, Abraham remained well, glad, and calmly happy. He knew his world might change in just a few minutes, but he still maintained his peace. He rejoiced in the Lord always and again he rejoiced. Even though Isaac's life was at stake, Abraham was able to declare, "It is well."

He recognized that if God needed to raise Isaac from the dead to keep His promise, then that's what He would do. Abraham staggered not at the promises of God but was strong in faith, giving glory to God. When you learn how to rejoice, you begin to understand why the Apostle Paul wrote, "For God hath not given us the spirit of fear; but of power, and of love, and of a sound mind" (2 Timothy 1:7).

Fear might be something difficult to overcome, but you can still rejoice in the midst of it. Worry might be hard to get past, but with the knowledge that God has all power, you can still declare, "It is well."

I am echoing the words of the Apostle Paul so that we can begin laying the foundation in our spirits to abstain from all appearance of evil. If you are simply trying to abstain from evil in your own flesh, you will not succeed. You will fall headlong into it. However, if you take the time to lay a proper foundation, then by the time you reach verse 22, you will be able to abstain without issue. You will abstain through the power of the Holy Spirit. The Holy Spirit will come upon you and enable you to abstain. The foundation must be laid correctly. The first layer that Paul laid is that we should rejoice evermore.

A GOOD REPORT

How do we learn to rejoice? We learn to rejoice as Jethro did—by hearing and receiving a good report. A good report generates rejoicing within you.

If we are truly going to live for the Lord as He desires, we cannot be satisfied with vague concepts and ideas. As my pastor used to say, we need to get down to where the rubber meets the road. Let's take this teaching into our daily lives. We must surround ourselves with people who give good reports.

Stop spending time with those who won't talk about God. Avoid those who speak of God but do so with a carnal distortion. Remember, the serpent in the Garden of Eden spoke about God as though he were a master on the subject, but his words were twisted by evil. Refuse to gather with individuals or groups who only offer negative, fleshly, or human reports.

Do not entertain conversations with people who only want to complain. I refuse to seek out conversations—especially when I need encouragement—with those who only want to lament their situation in life yet never take the time to seek a solution through prayer and reading the Word of the Lord.

I once attended a church service where the preacher asked the congregation, "Whose report will you believe?" Almost on cue, the congregation shouted back, "The report of the Lord." Nothing can make you rejoice quite like the report of the Lord. It's the kind of experience where you walk into church feeling depressed and ready to throw in the towel. In fact, you're so discouraged that you feel like throwing in all the towels. You're at the point where you want to get a cannon and start launching towels! You're ready to quit, give up, give out, and give in.

But then, something happens. The moment you get in touch with someone who has been in the presence of God and has a good report to share, something inside of you is strengthened. It stirs up the gift that is within you. It begins to move, shake, and revive that thing the Lord placed in your soul when He first laid His hand on your life.

SHARING THE GOOD REPORT

This is why you should share a good report. Talk about what the Lord has done for you. What has the Lord demonstrated and revealed in your life about healing? What has He shown you about mercy? What did God give you in prayer? What new understanding of the blood of Jesus Christ has He revealed to you? It's just that simple. Talk about it. Share it. Tell it.

Don't be the one to say, "Well, they're so heavenly-minded, all they talk about is the Bible. All they do is brag about what God did for them. Don't they have anything else to say?" Maybe you should try doing what they're doing every once in a while. You might find that you complain less. You might find that you aren't so easily offended. You might even find that you're not so miserable.

If our minds are truly on Heaven, we will want to share a good report with someone. If our minds are on Heaven, we will also want to receive a good report from others. Truly, that is the only kind of report that heavenly-minded people have to share—a good report. That is the only kind of report we should be interested in spreading: the report of the Lord.

So, stop spreading negativity. Stop spreading that jaded point of view. Share the good report so that others may rejoice evermore and be strengthened.

Proverbs 15:30 tells us, "The light of the eyes rejoiceth the heart: and a good report maketh the bones fat." The phrase "light of the eyes" refers to a person's cheerful countenance. When someone approaches you with a bright and cheerful expression and says, "God is good. Let me tell you what I mean," receive what they are saying. God is giving you a reason to rejoice, and we are instructed to "rejoice with them that rejoice."

Some people find it easier to weep with those who weep, and it can be a tactic of the enemy to make God's chosen people share only in sorrow and not in joy. If we are going to be united, let us be united on both fronts. If we truly believe in Oneness, we should be one in weeping with those who weep and one in rejoicing with those who rejoice.

Even if you don't have a good report to share from this year, reach back into the past and say, "God has been good. Let me tell you what I mean." Even if it's not your own testimony, but someone else shared it with you and it strengthened you, tell it anyway. The person you're speaking to might need that good report. And if you can't think of anything, speak the report of the Lord. You need to share that good report so that others can rejoice. When they hear it, it will help them to be well, to be glad, and to be calmly happy.

And as you speak it, it will help you as well. It doesn't matter what you are feeling in that moment—learn to speak the good report. I've learned that regardless of what is happening around me, speaking the good report can cause my spirit to rejoice. The report of the Lord will strengthen bones that were once brittle. Where they could easily have been broken before, now they are fortified and strengthened at the sound of the good report.

OVERCOMING OFFENSE

We often call it irritability. Someone glances in your direction and rolls their eyes. They don't realize you saw it, but now you're offended. It's our brittle bones—our fragile spirits—that cause us to react this way. Someone makes a snide remark, and we immediately think, "Oh, I am offended." We have become so easily offended in this day and age that I believe some of God's people will have more difficulty staying blameless and pure from the defilement of bitterness and offense than anything else they face in life.

If this describes you, then you need a good report. You need a fellow saint of God to come alongside you and remind you that He brought you out of darkness and into His marvelous light. We ought to take time throughout the day to remind ourselves of where we were when God found us. Many of us were not sitting on a church pew. Some were down and out, some were busted and broke, and others saw their lives shatter and fall apart around them. Yet, God, who is rich in mercy, reached way down into the muck and the mire and lifted us out of darkness, giving us a reason to rejoice. A good report like that will stir up rejoicing from even the most burdened soul.

I love to hear the saints of God talk about where they were when Jesus lifted them. They never could have imagined some of the places they found themselves or the things they were doing before He found them. It reminds me of the prodigal son. Picture him back in the father's house, wearing the best robe. In my estimation, someone grabbed one of the father's robes—the master of the house surely had the finest garments. The prodigal son is now adorned with a ring on his finger and new sandals on his feet. You would never guess that just a few months ago, he was about to eat with the pigs, having squandered all that his father had given him on reckless living.

But there he was, wallowing with the swine, far from home—until he came to himself. It was the reminder of the provision in his father's house that made him decide to go back. The uncovering of that good report, buried by the circumstances of his life, was enough to get him up and moving toward safety and security. It's that kind of report that makes brittle bones strong and causes the heart to rejoice. When you hear a report like that, it brings joy to your heart. It strengthens you. It makes you say, "I can rejoice in the Lord again."

Every once in a while, you need to speak a good report to the person you see in the mirror every day. It should be a weekly, if not daily, practice to remind yourself of where you were when God saved you. I'm telling you from experience: you can overcome offense by speaking a good report to yourself. The reports of this temporary world are just that—temporary. If you listen to them long enough, they can depress you. But remember this: even the trial you're going through right now is temporary. You can bank on that. So, don't dwell on it.

I know it might sound like telling someone who is stressed not to stress out, but it's crucial to understand that your trial is not permanent. Let the Lord help you look past it to the joy that is set before you. Build your hope on things eternal. Hold to God's unchanging hand. Rejoice evermore. Do not let anything derail your rejoicing in the Lord. Believe the report of the Lord, and you will truly understand how to rejoice. If you're struggling to rejoice, do it like the elders did: Count your blessings. Name them one by one.

FAITH AND GOOD REPORTS

We are laying the foundation for blamelessness. Blamelessness will come when you truly abstain from all appearance of evil. Let's turn our attention to Hebrews 11. This chapter features many of the Bible's characters that we hold near and dear to our hearts. Their lives and experiences took place long before our time, serving as examples of men and women of faith. They teach us how to truly rejoice. We won't go through this chapter verse by verse, but I do want to highlight a few key points.

Hebrews 11:1-2 says, "Now faith is the substance of things hoped for, the evidence of things not seen. For by it the elders obtained a good report." By what? By faith. The elders obtained a good report by faith. How do you obtain a good report? What if there is no one around to tell you how God cleaned them up, washed them up, and transformed their life? What if you don't have anyone near you sharing a good report? How do you obtain one then? You obtain a good report the same way the elders did—by faith. It was by faith that the elders received a good report. You obtain it by faith. You get it the way they got it.

Hebrews 11:3 states, "Through faith we understand that the worlds were framed by the word of God, so that things which are seen were not made of things which do appear." You might ask, "How do you know that the worlds were framed by the Word of God?" Through faith. People can mock it, but faith will move mountains. They can scoff at it, but I will hold onto it, even if the world is on fire around me. It doesn't matter to me who mocks or scoffs because this faith I have is precious to me.

THE POWER OF FAITH

The most important thing passed down to me in life had nothing to do with material possessions; it had everything to do with faith. Not a single material possession carried me through any trial in my life, but faith carried me through all of them. No family connection brought me through a fiery trial, but faith in my great God did. It was faith in the power of the blood of Jesus Christ. It was faith in the power of the Holy Ghost. You want a good report so that you can rejoice? You get it by faith.

I remember a time when I was under a severe spiritual weight. I was depressed. I was discouraged. With time and distance, I came to understand that it was the enemy of my soul coming against me with an evil report. In that moment, however, I didn't understand why I felt the way I did. I felt so low. To make matters worse, I was about to walk into a meeting that would determine a major shift in my family and our ministry. I was not in a good place. I had no desire to go into this meeting feeling this way, but nothing I was doing at the time was helping to lift the heavy depression.

Finally, I realized what was going on. This was a moment of mental clarity. Emotionally, I still felt beaten down and downtrodden. Mentally, I recognized that I was dealing with a demonic spirit.

Emotionally, I felt useless and worthless. But mentally, I understood that this was an evil spirit at work.

I didn't come to this realization on my own. It was my wife, Alayna, who helped me understand what I was dealing with spiritually. She came into the room with a good report. While I was feeling down on myself, wallowing in my despair, her countenance was bright. She spoke a simple yet powerful truth of God. She said, "God has been good. Why don't you go pray about it?"

What she said might seem obvious now, but in that moment—with the dilemma staring me in the face, and the spirit of depression breathing down my neck, pulling me into a place of despair—I didn't know what to do. I give myself a facepalm now because prayer should have been the first thing I did, yet it was the last thing I turned to.

However, there was something about what Alayna told me that gave me enough clarity to recognize what was happening and what I needed to do to get out of it. It was like a ray of light shining through the keyhole of a door. Her good report of God's goodness broke into my world where I felt trapped and showed me the way out.

So, I went and found a place of prayer. The moment I stepped into that prayer closet, the Lord was already waiting for me. I immediately felt His presence surround me. I lifted my voice and said, "Lord, You are good. I thank You for everything You have done in my life." I began to praise Him. I began to worship Him. I was rejoicing even before I fully understood what rejoicing meant. The more I thanked Him, the more the weight lifted. The more I rejoiced, the more the peace of God washed over my soul. The more I rejoiced, the more confident I became in His Word. The more I rejoiced, the more I understood that the Lord was still with me. I got up from that place of prayer speaking and believing, "It is well with my soul. God's got this."

To make a long story short, the meeting I went into could have easily compounded my depression with fear and anger. The meeting was essentially someone delivering a multitude of other people's negative reports. Yet, even as I listened to these bad reports, my spirit still rejoiced. As I sat there, hearing one negative report after another, I felt my body sink deeper into a relaxed position as the peace of God washed over me once again. I left that meeting with a happy calm flooding my soul, saying, "It is well. God's still got this."

In His Word, we are told, "Faith comes by hearing and hearing by the word of the Lord." The elders mentioned in Hebrews 11 did not receive the promise during their lifetimes. They saw it from a distance and understood they would not obtain it on this earth. Yet, by faith, they received it and held on to the good report that was delivered to them. Adversity arose in their lives, but by faith, they obtained, and by faith, they persevered. They faced betrayal, oppression, persecution, and many hardships, but through faith, they clung to the good report of the Lord. When you have a good report that you refuse to let go of, you can rejoice no matter the situation you find yourself in.

CHAPTER 3

SWEET HOUR OF PRAYER

A LIFE SATURATED WITH PRAYER

In 1 Thessalonians 5:17, the apostle Paul laid out the second level of the foundation for preparing Christians to abstain from all appearance of evil: "Pray without ceasing." This simple but profound command is not just advice but an essential discipline for overcoming the appearance of evil and living in constant communion with God. Paul essentially says, "I am teaching you how to abstain from all appearance of evil, and the way you do that is by praying without ceasing."

We must recognize that this is not just about making prayer a part of our lives—it is about making prayer our entire life. This is not a call for occasional prayer or ritualistic prayer, but for a life overwhelmed, consumed, and saturated with prayer. To live a life of prayer is to be immersed in constant communication with God, letting prayer flow through every moment and every action.

Prayer is more than a task; it is communion with God. If we remember the book of Genesis, the paradise called the Garden of

Eden was not just special because of its beauty. What made the garden such a special place for Adam and Eve was its communion with God. In the garden, they experienced unbroken fellowship with their Creator. Today, prayer is our way of returning to that paradise—a momentary taste of heaven on earth.

While we understand that heaven will be literal paradise, prayer gives us access, even for a brief moment, to that same communion here on earth. The more we pray, the more we align ourselves with God's Spirit. As we grow in prayer, we develop an intimate closeness with God, which in turn helps us better avoid the appearance of evil. This spiritual intimacy is not something that happens occasionally—it comes through a life of constant, ceaseless prayer.

THE CHALLENGE OF PRAYING WITHOUT CEASING

For many, the idea of praying without ceasing can seem overwhelming. It's easy to feel like there isn't enough time in the day to pray constantly, especially when our lives are filled with responsibilities, work, and the demands of everyday living. Our minds, through a lack of discipline, often struggle to stay focused in prayer. The concept of ceaseless prayer can seem like an impossible task when we're already struggling to find time for daily devotion.

There is another reason why this idea can feel intimidating: we have, in many ways, sensationalized prayer. Much like the Pharisees that Jesus warned about, we have made prayer something grandiose. We think it has to be something public or elaborate—like a performance before God or before others. But Jesus' instruction is simple. In Matthew 6:6, He tells us to go into our closet, to pray in secret, and that the Father who sees what is done in secret will reward us openly. Prayer is not about impressing others or fulfilling some religious obligation—it is about honest, heartfelt communion with God.

It is also important to recognize the necessity of prayer in every aspect of our lives. Prayer should precede every decision we make. We should not walk into a meeting, have an important conversation, or make a significant decision without first seeking God's guidance in prayer. Personally, I have experienced the transformative power of prayer in my own life. There have been moments when I knew that if I had entered a situation without first praying, my emotions and flesh would have taken over. But because I prayed beforehand, the Holy Spirit took control—bridling my tongue, directing my emotions, and guiding my thoughts. That is the power of prayer.

When we walk into situations with prayer, we aren't relying solely on our own mental faculties or wisdom—we are walking in the power of the Spirit. Imagine walking into a meeting or a difficult conversation not merely with your natural abilities but operating in the gifts of the Spirit, such as wisdom or knowledge. When you pray without ceasing, you allow God to work through you, empowering you to handle situations in ways that you could never manage on your own.

THE MISCONCEPTION OF RESTRICTING SPIRITUAL GIFTS

There is a common misconception that the gifts of the Spirit only operate during church services, as though they are reserved for Sunday mornings or midweek gatherings. But are we not believers outside of those times? The truth is that the gifts of the Spirit are meant to operate in our daily lives, not just within the walls of the church. When we walk in the Spirit, we experience the operation of these gifts constantly, regardless of where we are.

Prayer sensitizes us to the movement of the Holy Spirit. It opens our spiritual ears and eyes, enabling us to see and hear what God is doing in the world around us. When we are constantly in prayer, we walk in the Spirit, and as a result, we do not fulfill the desires of the flesh (Galatians 5:16). This kind of sensitivity to the Spirit's leading is essential for helping us to abstain from all appearance of evil.

Still, some believers struggle with prayer because they feel inadequate. They think they are not "spiritual enough" or don't know enough to pray effectively. But if you have the Holy Spirit, you are already empowered to pray. Jesus promised in Acts 1:8 that "you will receive power when the Holy Spirit comes on you." You don't need special training or qualifications to pray without ceasing. You already have the Holy Spirit, and through Him, you have the power to pray continuously.

PRAYER IS PERSONAL

It's also important to remember that prayer is not a competition. Sometimes, we feel intimidated by those who seem to pray more eloquently or confidently than we do. But we must remember that prayer is a personal communion between you and God. It's not about the words you say or the length of your prayer—it's about the sincerity of your heart. If something weighs on your heart, bring it to God. Prayer is as simple as sharing the burdens of your heart with the Lord, trusting Him to intervene in every situation.

Jesus warns us in Matthew 6:7 against vain repetitions in prayer. He tells us not to pray like the heathens, who believe they will be heard because of their many words. Vain repetitions are empty words spoken out of obligation, not out of a sincere heart. But Jesus offers us a model for prayer in The Lord's Prayer (Matthew 6:9-13). This prayer is not meant to be a script that we mindlessly recite, but rather a guide for how to pray from the heart—focusing on God's will, His provision, His forgiveness, and His deliverance.

When you pray from the heart, God hears you. It doesn't matter whether you've been serving the Lord for decades or just starting your journey—when your prayer comes from a sincere heart, it reaches the throne of God. He hears the cry of your soul, and He responds.

DEVELOPING A CONSISTENT PRAYER LIFE

Building a consistent prayer life takes time, discipline, and intentionality. For some, a structured prayer routine can be helpful. There are prayer plans like the Tabernacle Prayer Plan or extended versions of The Lord's Prayer that can guide your time in prayer and help you develop a deeper, more focused prayer life. These tools can be especially helpful for those who are new to consistent prayer or those looking to deepen their prayer habits.

However, while structured prayer routines can be helpful, it's important not to become so reliant on them that you lose sensitivity to the Holy Spirit. There will be days when prayer flows naturally, and other days when it feels like a struggle. On those difficult days, it may help to enter God's presence with worship. As Psalm 100:2 tells us, "Come before His presence with singing." Singing praises can soften your heart and prepare you for deeper communion with God.

In the process of developing a prayer life, we begin to experience more of the fruit of the Spirit in our lives. As we pray, we cultivate spiritual fruit, and as the fruit of the Spirit grows, the gifts of the Spirit also begin to flow through us.

THE POWER OF INTERCESSORY PRAYER

One of the most powerful forms of prayer is intercessory prayer, where we pray not for ourselves, but for others. The Bible tells us in Job 42:10 that the Lord turned the captivity of Job when he prayed for his friends. When we pray for others with the same intensity and desperation that we would pray for ourselves, miracles happen. Intercession is a form of prayer where God prays through us, and when God prays, things get done.

When you engage in intercessory prayer, you step into the supernatural realm, where time seems to stop, and the power of God flows through you. In those moments, God works through your prayers to bring healing, deliverance, and miracles into the lives of others.

The world needs more intercessors. There is a noticeable lack of the miraculous when there are no intercessors. But when believers rise up to pray for others, powerful things begin to happen. If you feel compassion or empathy for someone while you're praying, take that as a sign to intercede for them. Pray for them as if you were praying for yourself, and watch how God moves on their behalf.

SPIRITUAL WARFARE AND THE ARMOR OF GOD

Ephesians 6:10-18 instructs us to put on the whole armor of God because we are not wrestling against flesh and blood but against spiritual forces of evil. The armor of God equips us for battle, but prayer is the means by which we put that armor into action. Without prayer, we are not ready for the spiritual battles we face daily. Through prayer, the breastplate of righteousness, the shield of faith, the helmet of salvation, and the sword of the Spirit are secured in place, empowering us to stand firm against the enemy's attacks.

Paul's instruction in Ephesians 6:18, "praying always with all prayer and supplication in the Spirit," emphasizes the importance of prayer in every aspect of life. Whether it's group prayer, individual prayer, silent prayer, or fervent prayer, we must continually seek God's guidance and strength. It is through prayer that the armor of God becomes active in our lives, enabling us to stand strong in spiritual warfare.

A prayerless Christian, though perhaps clothed in the armor of God, accomplishes little because they have not entered the battle through prayer. Prayer is the key to spiritual victory. Without it, we are powerless in the face of the enemy's attacks. Winston Churchill once said that overconfidence leading to neglect and slothfulness is one of the worst crimes in wartime. The same is true in spiritual warfare. We must not be overconfident in our own abilities—we must rely on the power of prayer to win the spiritual battles we face.

THE POWER OF UNCEASING PRAYER

When we pray without ceasing, we allow God's Spirit to lead and guide every moment of our lives. We no longer rely on our own abilities, but we trust in the faithfulness of God to direct our steps and protect us from evil. This is the essence of walking in the Spirit—allowing God to take control and guide us according to His will.

As Paul reminds us in 1 Thessalonians 5, "Faithful is He that calleth you, who also will do it." God is faithful to protect us, guide us, and help us overcome temptation. But it requires that we live a life of prayer—a life of continuous, unceasing communion with Him. When we submit to God in prayer, He is faithful to preserve us blameless until the coming of our Lord Jesus Christ.

Whether you are praying for yourself, for others, or interceding on behalf of those in need, never stop praying. Prayer is the lifeline that connects us to God's power, wisdom, and guidance. When we pray without ceasing, we not only abstain from the appearance of evil, but we walk in victory, empowered by the Holy Spirit to overcome every challenge and fulfill God's will in our lives.

CHAPTER 4

GIVE THANKS, IN THIS?

THE POWER OF THANKSGIVING IN TRIALS

The next layer that the Apostle Paul laid down for the believer is that we give thanks in everything. Thanksgiving. Let's make something clear right now: when we reach Thanksgiving Day, it's not "Turkey Day." It's Thanksgiving Day. It's not about the turkey; it's about giving God thanks.

I'm reminded of the beautiful song, Thanks, Thanks. It goes, "Thanks, thanks. I give you thanks for all you've done. I am so blessed. My soul has found rest. O Lord, I give you thanks." Did you know that Rev. Carroll McGruder wrote that song while pacing the floor of his kitchen in the middle of the night, battling a terrible cancer diagnosis? Chemotherapy had taken its toll on his body, and during this struggle, he woke up to the adversarial voice of Satan saying, "You should be afraid. You're going to lose your life. God has forsaken you. I'm going to take your life."

Instead of giving in to that voice, he began to give God thanks.

He put pen to paper and wrote, "I am so blessed. My soul has found rest." Do you say those kinds of things when you're standing on top of the mountain? Isn't that the type of praise that comes easily when everything is going just the way you prefer? But do you still say those things when cancer is ravaging your body, threatening to take you away from your family? Is that when you give thanks? Absolutely. You give God thanks in everything, because this is the will of God in Christ Jesus concerning you.

That statement is so powerful—this is the will of God concerning you. If you've ever needed to know the will of God, you can know it today. You don't have to look any further in Scripture than right here. In everything, give thanks. If God can transform you into a person who gives thanks in every circumstance, that's the will of God at work in your life.

If God can take you from being a grumbler, a complainer, a murmurer, or a doubter, and transform you into a grateful and thankful child of God, His will is being fulfilled in you. If God can take you from groaning and moaning about everything to being truly thankful in all seasons and places, that is the will of God coming to pass in your life.

THE DIFFERENCE BETWEEN "IN" AND "FOR"

Let's revisit this preposition in verse 18 because it begins with a crucial word: IN. Let's be clear about what it's not saying. It does not say to give thanks for everything that happens. If your pet cat gets hit by a car and ends up with a cast on her leg, you don't have to thank God for little Mittens getting hurt. But you do need to thank God in the midst of dealing with that struggle. IN, not FOR.

"In everything give thanks, for this is the will of God in Christ Jesus concerning you." If you receive a report that shakes you or doesn't sit well, you don't need to give thanks for the report. But you should give thanks in the middle of the circumstance that brought you that report.

Now, how do we give God thanks? Let's talk about that. First of all, it needs to come from our mouths. But before it can come from our mouths, it must first come from our hearts. As we've discussed previously, if it's not in your heart when it comes out of your mouth, it's meaningless. It becomes vain repetition if your heart isn't engaged. We don't want to say things we don't truly believe, but here's the catch-22: sometimes you struggle to believe it until you start confessing it.

There may be something you know is true, but you're not yet convinced in your heart. That's when you need to start confessing it with your mouth so your heart can follow. This is why the Bible says in Romans to "confess with your mouth and believe in your heart." People often think they can't confess something until they fully believe it in their hearts. But what if you reversed that? What if you said, "I know my heart needs to believe this because it is the truth. So, I will confess it with my mouth until my heart is persuaded by that truth. I'll confess it until my heart comes into order."

Remember, the heart is desperately wicked and deceitful above all things. You haven't encountered a devil more deceptive than your own heart. That's why you have to command your heart what to believe and be persuaded by. This is why James talks about having the tongue bridled by the Spirit of God. If you can bring the tongue under control, it will bring your body into order.

Here's what it looks like: "I believe that God is a healer." Confess it with your mouth. "I believe that God is the Savior." Confess it with your mouth. Even if you struggle to fully believe it, it doesn't make it any less true. Confess it anyway. If you start believing, there is nothing on this planet as powerful as a believer. When you start believing the words of praise that you're confessing, watch out—miracles will begin to flow in your wake. So, in everything, open your mouth and give God thanks.

We're blessed in ways we don't deserve. I don't know how it happened—someone much smarter than I could explain it—but somehow, in the middle of the night, God came down and kept my heart beating while I was asleep. That happens all the time, doesn't it? Exactly. But how often do we stop and thank Him for it? Not nearly enough.

While we were asleep, we weren't consciously thinking about it. We were just sawing logs, getting some good shut-eye. But while I was asleep, the Lord kept my lungs inhaling and exhaling. He kept my heart pumping blood throughout my body, circulating it just as needed. I didn't do that. I didn't have the presence of mind to make it happen. And even if I did, if my heart decided to stop beating right now, what could I do about it?

God has been so good to us. Why don't we just take a break from our problems and lift up a shout of praise to the Lord? Let's talk about how He saved us from our sins. Let's talk about how He redeemed us from our own destruction. Let's talk about how He reached way down into the pits we dug for ourselves—pits He didn't have to pull us out of, but He did anyway.

We broke every commandment. We broke every law. We transgressed so many times that we've lost count. We've defied His Word. We've snubbed Him, spurned Him, slighted Him, denied Him, and betrayed Him. Yet, His mercy reached down to sinners, of whom we are chief. While we were yet in sin, Christ died for the ungodly.

Here's how you can give God thanks in everything: you can always find something to thank Him for. "My car broke down." Thank Him that it ran as long as it did. "My air conditioner went out." Thank Him that it'll be working again soon enough. There's always something to be thankful for. "I've got an ache in my left leg." Thank Him that the ache isn't in both legs. You can always be thankful for something.

A WEAPON AGAINST TEMPTATION

Some may wonder what giving thanks has to do with abstaining from all appearance of evil and being preserved blameless. Here's the connection: when it comes time to abstain from all appearance of evil, if you've developed the habit of thanking God for every good and perfect gift, for every blessing He's given you, when you face temptation, you're more likely to stay loyal and faithful to Him.

Let me prove this to you scripturally. We see an example of this in the life of Joseph. When Potiphar's wife tempted Joseph, he ran from the temptation, and this is what he said: "How then can I do this great wickedness, and sin against God?" Joseph was a man who had learned to give thanks to God. In the prison? He gave thanks. In the pit? He gave thanks. Betrayed by his own brothers? He gave thanks. Sold into slavery? He gave thanks. Despised and rejected by his own family? He still gave thanks. So, when Potiphar's wife came calling, tempting and luring him, Joseph was more likely to remain faithful to God because he had cultivated the habit of saying, "Lord, I thank You."

Notice what the Psalmist says about praising the Lord: Psalm 150:1-2, "Praise ye the Lord. Praise God in His sanctuary: praise Him in the firmament of His power. Praise Him for His mighty acts: praise Him according to His excellent greatness."

If you're looking for something to praise Him for, here's where to start: praise Him for His mighty acts. Thank Him for parting the Red Sea, for delivering Daniel out of the lion's den, for saving the three Hebrew children from the fiery furnace. Praise Him for overshadowing Mary and bringing forth the only begotten Son of God, born under the Law. Praise Him because He gave His life so that whoever believes and obeys His Word will not perish but have everlasting life.

I've got some mighty acts to thank Him for. Thank Him for the night you were so intoxicated that you still don't know how you got home—but you did. Let me tell you how you got home: God never left you. He never forsook you. He kept you the whole time. You've got some things for which to be thankful. Give Him the praise that He deserves.

Now, let's talk about the word "excellent." We throw that word around so casually, like it's just another synonym for good, great, or wonderful. But it's so much more. EXCEL-lent. Excelling. His greatness excels. His greatness excels beyond the medication you're on right now. His greatness excels beyond the advice you've been given. His greatness excels beyond mine, yours, or anyone else's greatest achievements. His greatness excels above all things in this world. The more you praise Him and thank Him, the more likely you are to abstain from all appearance of evil.

God is faithful to us, and I am thankful for His faithfulness. He is so very faithful. Sometimes, like in the life of Job, the enemy comes around and tries to convince the Lord to remove the hedges He has placed around us. But God only allows it if it's for our good. He doesn't play games with our lives; He only permits it if it's something we need—and even then, it comes with conditions. The enemy comes to God and says, "Well, I can't do anything to him because of that hedge. Of course, he's going to live for you because you've left that hedge up." And the Lord responds, "I'll take that hedge down because there's more work to be done in his life. I'll remove it, but you can't take his life."

It always comes with conditions because God is faithful to us. That's why we're still here, praising His name. That's why we've made it this far. We should take a moment to look back on every time we've murmured or said, "I just don't think I can make it." How many times have I uttered that in my life? Only in glory will we know how often we mumbled, stammered, and grumbled, "I just don't think I can make it." Yet, here we are. We made it. Give Him thanks.

Let me remind you: we are Spirit-filled, Spirit-led, thanksgiving people of God. So when we give God thanks, we really give Him thanks. Our thanksgiving is manifested in our praise. We see this precedent in the Scriptures in the life of David. When he saw the ark of the covenant coming back to Israel, he gave God praise. Israel had been so careless, so complacent with the ark of the Lord, yet God, in His mercy, brought the ark back to them. When David saw that the Lord hadn't given up on Israel, he couldn't help but praise Him. He danced before the Lord. He gave thanks.

This wasn't something you saw every day, and you wouldn't see it in our day either. You wouldn't casually glance out the window and see a head of state, like the King of Israel, throwing caution to the wind and dancing before the Lord. It was so out of the ordinary. His wife, Michal, was embarrassed. She thought she knew how a king was supposed to act. After all, her father, Saul, had been king, and he certainly wouldn't have been caught dead out there dancing.

2 Samuel 6:20-23 says, "Then David returned to bless his household. And Michal the daughter of Saul came out to meet David, and

said, How glorious was the king of Israel today, who uncovered himself today in the eyes of the handmaids of his servants, as one of the vain fellows shamelessly uncovereth himself! And David said unto Michal, It was before the Lord, who chose me before thy father, and before all his house, to appoint me ruler over the people of the Lord, over Israel: therefore will I play before the Lord. And I will yet be more vile than thus, and will be base in mine own sight: and of the maidservants which thou hast spoken of, of them shall I be had in honour. Therefore Michal the daughter of Saul had no child unto the day of her death."

In other words, David was saying, "You have no idea what you're talking about. God has been too good to me for me not to praise His name. He's been so kind to me. I must praise His name."

As a minister of the gospel, I appreciate when people are praising, praying, worshiping, and giving thanks to God. The blood-washed multitude has a right to shout, "Worthy is the Lamb who purchased my salvation." There is power in that praise and in giving thanksgiving unto the Lord.

We see another example of this when Miriam and the daughters of Zion grabbed their tambourines and began to worship God. She's the one who showed us how to use a tambourine! Miriam began dancing, rejoicing, and lifting up the Lord in song. And you know, you would do the same thing if the Red Sea had just parted before your eyes. Imagine watching an army of malicious soldiers, who were coming to kill you, be drowned in the waters. Anyone left alive would have been dragged back to Egypt in chains. You'd do the same thing if you were standing there, thinking, "Alright, Moses, any time now!"

You'd do the same thing if, just when you thought all hope was lost, the God you so faithfully serve stood those waters up like walls on both sides, parted them so you could walk through on dry ground, and then brought them crashing down on the very army that sought to take your life. He let them enter the same territory just to crush them beneath the weight of the Red Sea. You better believe Miriam gave God thanks that day.

What would you do if you were in their place? Your emotions would be running high. You're thinking that you and your family are about to die. And then, suddenly, all of Israel is walking through on dry ground. But as you look back, you see the dust cloud from the Egyptian army, still pursuing you. You're moving, but so are they. The moment you reach the other side, the waters crash back down on them, and now you're thanking God because He is a mighty deliverer.

You wouldn't just look up and say, "Good job, God." No, you'd dance. You'd shout. You'd sing. You'd beat that tambourine because that's exactly what God did for you when He saved you from your sins.

Some people think that the praise and worship that goes on in church is just people caught up in a frenzy of emotion. Well, guess what? God made us to be emotional beings! So if you think it's emotion, you're absolutely right. When you know what the Lord has done for someone like you, you can't help but get emotional. I get emotional when I think about how far the Lord has brought me and all that He's brought me through. It gets into my hands, it gets into my feet.

But it's not just human emotion—it's more than that. The Lord inhabits the praises of His people. You can't read the Book of Psalms and come away thinking anything other than the fact that the Lord enjoys loud, emotional praise and worship. He likes it loud! He didn't say, "Make a joyful whisper." He said, "Make a joyful noise." He was clear: "Praise Him upon the loud cymbals, and upon the high-sounding cymbals." It's a shout of triumph!

Of course, the Apostle Paul taught us that not everyone will understand what's happening in a church service, so everything must be done decently and in order. Some people might walk in and leave thinking, "They've lost their minds." But when you truly understand what the blood of Jesus has done and what the Spirit of the Lord is doing, you sometimes just can't help it. In everything, give thanks, for this is the will of God in Christ Jesus concerning you. Have a thankful heart. Give praise with a thankful heart.

There are moments when I have to rebuke myself. I might start thinking about the challenges I'm facing, and then I look over at someone else and realize how blessed I am. We all go through seasons of struggle and difficulty, but somehow, God keeps us. He wraps His arms around us, holds us in His hands, and sustains us through those tough seasons. Sometimes I just have to stop and say, "Lord, thank You. Thank You for keeping me. Thank You for keeping my family. Thank You for keeping my marriage. Thank You for ordering my steps." It's not by our own strength—it's the Lord who has done this. We are His people and the sheep of His pasture. It is He who has made us, and not we ourselves.

Psalm 100:1-5, Make a joyful noise unto the LORD, all ye lands. 2. Serve the LORD with gladness: come before His presence with singing. 3. Know ye that the LORD He is God: it is He that hath made us, and not we ourselves; we are His people, and the sheep of His pasture. 4. Enter into His gates with thanksgiving, and into His courts with praise: be thankful unto Him, and bless His name. 5. For the LORD is good; His mercy is everlasting; and His truth endureth to all generations."

Let's take a closer look at this because I know how some of us think. We might read this as a call to praise, worship, and thank Him when we go to church during the week. If the music isn't too loud, we'll thank Him. If the preacher keeps the message short, we'll send a thank you to the Lord. If there's food after the service, we're definitely thankful! I've even started noticing when I say, "I'm coming to a close," I hear some people say, a little louder than usual, "Oh, thank you, Jesus." I used to think they were just praising God, but I'm starting to make the connection!

While it certainly means giving thanks during a church service, that's not all it means. "Enter into His gates with thanksgiving" means that whenever you need to enter His presence, you can do it with a thankful heart. It doesn't matter where you are, geographically or spiritually—thank Him. You could be staring down the gates of hell, with evil surrounding you and threatening to overwhelm you, but if you thank God in that moment, you'll find yourself entering the Lord's gates instead.

You might be sitting in a hospital, with spirits of fear dancing around you and doubt taunting you, but if you give God thanks right there, you'll enter His gates. Not just any gates—the gates of pearl, the gates of His majesty, the gates of His presence and kingdom. You'll be sitting in the hospital, but spiritually, you'll be seated in heavenly places with Christ Jesus. The key to those gates opening is thanksgiving. Wherever you are, give Him thanks, and you can enter in.

Did you know that you can pray for something for so long and with such intensity that, when God answers, you're so caught up in the miracle that you might forget to thank Him? A classic example of this is the miracle of the ten lepers, as recorded in Luke 17:12-19, And as he entered into a certain village, there met him ten men that were lepers, which stood afar off: 13. And they lifted up their voices, and said, Jesus, Master, have mercy on us. 14. And when he saw them, he said unto them, Go shew yourselves unto the priests. And it came to pass, that, as they went, they were cleansed. 15. And one of them, when he saw that he was healed, turned back, and with a loud voice glorified God, 16. And fell down on his face at his feet, giving him thanks: and he was a Samaritan. 17. And Jesus answering said, Were there not ten cleansed? but where are the nine? 18. There are not found that returned to give glory to God, save this stranger. 19. And he said unto him, Arise, go thy way: thy faith hath made thee whole.

Jesus healed all ten lepers. The Bible tells us that they all went on their way rejoicing, but one, a Samaritan leper, stopped and thought, "Wait a minute. What are we doing?" He turned back to say, "Thank you." Something happened for him that didn't happen for the others. Jesus not only healed him but made him whole. The others were healed, meaning that the leprosy in their bodies had been stopped. The disease had been cured, and no more damage would be done. But this one man, because he returned to give thanks, was made whole. The effects of leprosy weren't just halted—they were reversed. He was restored completely.

RESTORATION IN THANKSGIVING

This shows us that thanksgiving begins to reverse the effects of sin in our lives. Thanksgiving takes us back over our past, beginning to heal and restore what has been scarred by sin. You may still remember the pain of what you went through, but when you thank God, He makes you whole. You start living like you never went through those moments. There is a restorative power in thanksgiving. When you're made whole, you're made blameless. He sanctifies us wholly— our spirit, soul, and body. As you thank God, you'll find yourself thanking Him for things you never thought you would. The Apostle Paul calls it, "Count it all joy." You'll reach a place in the Spirit where you'll count it all joy.

Matthew 5:8, "Blessed are the pure in heart: for they shall see God." Those who are pure in heart see God in everything. It doesn't matter if it's bad, good, or ugly—they still see God. There have been traumatic moments in my past that, for a long time, I couldn't even bring myself to think about. But when I let the Lord into those areas, He healed me. As I felt His healing power wash over me, I began to thank Him. And because I thanked Him, He didn't just heal me—He made me whole. Now, those moments are part of my testimony of what God can do in someone's life. I see the handiwork of God in those rough seasons. They were fierce, ugly, and enough to cripple my life, but when I gave Him thanks, He purified me. Now, I can see the beauty that came from it.

I know it can be so bad, so ugly, that it seems like no good could ever come from it. But watch God go to work. In fact, thank Him for it right now. Start saying, "Lord, I don't know how this is going to work out, but I know You well enough to know that You're not done with this yet. I give You praise right now for every soul that will be positively impacted by what I'm going through. I thank You right now for every life that's going to be changed because of this fiery trial."

I know it can seem so bad and so ugly that you could never dream of any good coming from it, but watch God go to work. In fact, thank Him for it now. Right now. Start saying, "Lord, I don't know how this is going to work out, but I know You well enough to know that You're not done with this yet. I give You praise right now for every soul that will be positively impacted because of what I'm going through. I thank You now for every life that's going to be changed because of this fiery trial." In everything, give thanks.

Philippians 4:11-13, "Not that I speak in respect of want: for I have learned, in whatsoever state I am, therewith to be content. I know both how to be abased, and I know how to abound: every where and in all things I am instructed both to be full and to be hungry, both to abound and to suffer need. I can do all things through Christ which strengtheneth me."

CONTENTMENT THROUGH THANKSGIVING

Notice what the Apostle Paul says in Philippians 4: "Not that I speak in respect of want: for I have learned…" Some people go through seasons of difficulty so that they have the opportunity to testify about what they have learned from the Lord. You might have multiple accomplishments that you can show as life experience, but nothing can teach you like what the fiery trial can teach you. By the help of God, you're going to come out of this and say, as Paul did, "I have learned."

Paul had learned to be content no matter what state he was in at that particular moment of life. This meant being content even while holding on to a broken piece of a ship. He should have been preaching on Mars Hill, but instead, he was floating in the ocean because a nautical expert said it was safe to sail through the storm. He was subjected to a ship-sinking storm because of someone else's mistake and decision, but he learned something in the process. He learned, regardless of his current state, to be content.

You can approach difficulty in one of two ways: through your flesh, or through the Spirit. If you go through the flesh, it will become contentious. If you go through the Spirit, it will become contentment. It goes back to rejoicing evermore. It is well. Hold your peace and let the Lord fight your battle. I'm content. I have learned that in whatsoever state I am**, therewith to be content.

Paul says, "I know both how to be abased, and I know how to abound." My suffering and struggle—and thanking God through it—taught me how to be content when I am abased. Abased means having the foundation knocked from under you. Base without. Base removed. Paul said, "Because I have thanked God through my struggles, I have learned how to be content when I am abased, and I have learned how to be content when I abound."

We're not always ready for that. Because what do we do when we start abounding? When compliments are abundant, when money is abundant, when good times and good friends are abundant? Do we even need contentment anymore? Wrong. Thanking God for the little things you have in the struggle teaches you how to be content even when you are abounding.

Paul tells us that he has been instructed by God to know both to be full and to be hungry (Philippians 4:12). This is a level of spiritual maturity. If you can grasp it, you are one step closer to being able to genuinely abstain from all appearance of evil and be preserved blameless until the coming of our Lord Jesus Christ. I know how to be full and to be hungry.

The Queen of Sheba came from the uttermost parts of the earth to witness the wisdom of Solomon. Whatever drew her from where she was must have been extraordinary. She brought a caravan full of treasures, but when she arrived and saw Solomon's wisdom, the Bible says there was no more spirit in her—it took her breath away. She exclaimed, "Howbeit I believed not the words, until I came, and mine eyes had seen it: and, behold, the half was not told me: thy wisdom and prosperity exceedeth the fame which I heard" (1 Kings 10:7).

The wisdom she had heard about was only half of the story, but that was enough to compel her to make the journey. Once she saw it for herself, she realized that there was another half—something beyond words, something that had to be experienced. This is how the Word of God and the power of the Gospel work. There is a half that can be told, a half that compels people to come and experience God. But there is another half—the half that cannot be told, that can only be experienced personally.

When the Apostle Paul said, "I am instructed both to be full and to be hungry," he was pointing to something that cannot merely be taught—it has to be lived through, experienced. Only God can take you through the process of being both full and hungry at the same time. This understanding comes through struggles and sufferings in life, and it comes through thanksgiving. If you start thanking Him now, even in difficult times, the things of this world will grow strangely dim in the light of His glory. You will know how to be both full and yet still hungry for more of God. If He never did another thing for me, I am full. Yet, I can't wait to see what He does next.

Philippians 4:11-12 says, "Not that I speak in respect of want: for I have learned, in whatsoever state I am, therewith to be content. I know both how to be abased, and I know how to abound: every where and in all things I am instructed both to be full and to be hungry, both to abound and to suffer need."

I pray that every believer reaches a place in their walk with God where they learn to be content in whatever state they are in, just as Paul described. This is a profound revelation that all believers need to grasp. But Paul gives us the key to this contentment in the very next verse: "I can do all things through Christ which strengtheneth me" (Philippians 4:13).

We are all ready to go to heaven, but as long as the Lord tarries, He still has a harvest to bring in. Paul described being with Jesus as gain, and he defined godliness in his letter to Timothy: "Without controversy, great is the mystery of godliness: God was manifest in the flesh, justified in the Spirit, seen of angels, preached unto the Gentiles, believed on in the world, received up into glory" (1 Timothy 3:16). Jesus is godliness—the life, death, and resurrection of Jesus, the work of His blood, His Spirit, and His Word are all godliness. And heaven is gain.

Paul also wrote, "Godliness with contentment is great gain" (1 Timothy 6:6). If you can be content knowing that His grace is sufficient for you, that His blood has the power to heal, and that the promise of the Holy Spirit is for you and your children—then you are already as close to heaven as you can be on this earth. This is the great mystery of godliness: being content in the power and promises of God.

I told you earlier about the song Brother Carroll McGruder wrote during his battle with cancer. Some of the greatest worship songs have been written in the heat of fiery trials. That's why those old songs resonate so deeply—they come from a place of genuine struggle and thanksgiving. Paul and others like him learned lessons in those trials, and they wrote songs of praise and thanksgiving. Not everyone has the talent to write a worship song or sing beautifully, but every one of us has a song of thanksgiving we can offer. We all have a story, a testimony.

Put your life, your past, present, and future in God's hands. Yield your body, your mind, and your spirit to Him. Let Him make beautiful music with your life. Give Him thanks in everything, and let that song of thanksgiving ring out again and again. This is the will of God in Christ Jesus concerning you: In everything, give thanks!

CHAPTER 5

LET GO AND LET GOD

I remember attending a church conference some time ago, where a powerful, life-altering move of the Holy Ghost took place during one particular service. It wasn't just your typical Sunday night service; this was one of those moments that forever shifts the atmosphere, that pierces your heart, and challenges your very perception of what God is able to do. I saw people who came in burdened by life's struggles leave completely transformed, tears of joy streaming down their faces.

It all started simply. The minister leading the service—he didn't put on any airs or make a big production—just a sincere request: "Let's all give God our most heartfelt praise." It was in that moment, as our voices lifted in unity, that the Holy Ghost descended on us like a mighty wind. The entire congregation was arrested by the presence of the Spirit, and the atmosphere shifted into something otherworldly. It felt like heaven had opened up over that auditorium.

As I stood there, caught up in the glory of God's presence, I noticed that the leaders of the conference were quietly discussing how to proceed. As much as they were enjoying this powerful move of the Spirit, they were intent on making sure the Word of the Lord was preached. I watched as they decided to make a gentle transition. The ushers began moving, picking people up from the floor and guiding them back to their seats.

The conference organizers then called a brother up to sing a song. It was their way of signaling to the congregation that the preacher was about to take the pulpit. Looking back, I find some humor in that situation—being the one called upon to transition a service from this profound move of the Spirit to a structured time for preaching. I imagined the conversation: "Brother, if we ever needed you, we need you now. Come up here and stop the Holy Ghost from moving any further."

Of course, that wasn't what was truly happening. But in the moment, it struck me how delicate these transitions are in a service. The Word of God was going to be preached, but the Spirit was moving mightily in the praise, and in reality, there's no better way to transition into the preaching of the Word than through intense worship.

This leads us to why the Apostle Paul instructs that everything be done decently and in order (1 Corinthians 14:40). There is a balance between structure and allowing the Spirit to move. While we must ensure the Word is preached, we also must be sensitive not to quench the Spirit in our personal lives or in our gatherings.

THE SPIRIT ON THE MOVE

Our first encounter with the Spirit of God in Scripture happens all the way back in Genesis 1:1-2: In the beginning God created the heaven and the earth. And the earth was without form, and void; and darkness was upon the face of the deep. And the Spirit of God moved upon the face of the waters.*

Think about this scene for a moment. The earth is without form, void, and covered in darkness. There is no life, no movement—until the Spirit of God begins to hover over the waters. Just as the Spirit of God brought order to creation, the Holy Ghost works in our lives to bring order to the chaos of sin, to give life where there was once only emptiness.

I'm reminded of how often we ask God to "move" in our situations. We've all said it, haven't we? "I need God to move in this circumstance." "Lord, move upon their heart." Whether we realize it or not, we are describing the work of the Spirit. The Spirit of God is always moving, active, and dynamic. It's invisible to the naked eye, yet it carries immense power.

Jesus explained the movement of the Spirit further when He spoke to Nicodemus in John 3:1-7. Nicodemus came to Jesus, curious about the power behind the miracles He performed. Jesus told him plainly that "except a man be born of water and of the Spirit, he cannot enter into the kingdom of God." In this, Jesus was pointing out that there is a work of the Spirit that goes beyond human understanding. The Spirit is not only present at creation but is essential for our spiritual rebirth and transformation.

In John 3:8, Jesus likens the Spirit of God to the wind: "The wind bloweth where it listeth, and thou hearest the sound thereof, but canst not tell whence it cometh, and whither it goeth: so is every one that is born of the Spirit."

Here, Jesus gives us a powerful image to help us understand how the Spirit moves. You can feel the wind on your skin, see its effects as it rustles the leaves, but you can't control it, nor can you predict its movements. The same is true of the Spirit. It moves in ways we cannot fully comprehend, and we must allow it to move freely in our lives if we want to experience the fullness of its power.

THE DECEPTION IN THE AIRWAVES

It's interesting to note that after the fall of man, Satan is referred to as "the prince of the power of the air" (Ephesians 2:2). The enemy is always trying to imitate God's power and authority. Since the Spirit of God moves like the wind, Satan, too, seeks dominion over the air.

Have you ever noticed how much of our world's communication happens through the airwaves? Radio frequencies, television broadcasts, the internet—all of it is transmitted through the air. The enemy has capitalized on this, using media and communication to spread fear, confusion, and division.

Turn on the news for five minutes, and you'll see it. The enemy thrives on creating an atmosphere of fear and hopelessness. He's influencing the messages we hear, manipulating the airwaves to keep us distracted from the truth of God's Word. That's why it's so important to be discerning about what we allow into our minds and hearts.

However, even though Satan may be called the prince of the power of the air, I'm glad to know that there is still a **holy wind from heaven** that's at work. The Spirit of God is continually moving, and His power far exceeds anything the enemy can do. The wind of the Spirit can blow through the noise and confusion of this world, bringing peace, clarity, and direction to those who are listening.

THE SPIRIT LIKE WIND AND FIRE

We see this imagery of the wind again in the Book of Acts, during the outpouring of the Holy Ghost at Pentecost. Acts 2:1-4 tells us: "And when the day of Pentecost was fully come, they were all with one accord in one place. And suddenly there came a sound from heaven as of a rushing mighty wind, and it filled all the house where they were sitting."

Can you imagine being in that room, feeling the rush of the wind as the Holy Ghost fell? It wasn't just a gentle breeze; it was a mighty wind, filling every corner of the room and every heart present. But that wasn't the only image we are given of the Spirit that day. Acts 2:3-4 continues: "And there appeared unto them cloven tongues like as of fire, and it sat upon each of them. And they were all filled with the Holy Ghost, and began to speak with other tongues, as the Spirit gave them utterance."

Here, we see the Spirit described not only as wind but as fire. The tongues of fire rested upon each person, symbolizing the purifying and empowering work of the Holy Ghost. Fire refines, and the Spirit, like fire, purges us of sin, empowering us to live holy lives and carry out God's will.

THE TONGUE: YIELDED TO THE SPIRIT

When the Holy Ghost fell on the day of Pentecost, something remarkable happened. Those who were filled began to speak in other tongues as the Spirit gave them utterance. These weren't just random words—they were a direct result of the Spirit moving through them. Their human tongues, normally unruly and difficult to control, were now completely yielded to God.

It's important to understand that the Holy Ghost didn't physically move their tongues for them. No, these were still their own tongues, but now they were speaking words that only the Spirit could give. It was the human tongue being fully submitted to the divine will of God. This is what happens when we yield to the Spirit—it begins to work through us in ways that go far beyond our natural capabilities.

James talks about the power of the tongue, calling it an "unruly evil" that no man can tame. James 3:8 says, "But the tongue can no man tame; it is an unruly evil, full of deadly poison." If we're honest, we've all experienced the damage an unyielded tongue can do. We try to hold our peace, but then someone pushes our buttons, and we lash out. Words fly, cutting through the air like knives, leaving wounds that are hard to heal.

I've been there myself, struggling to control my tongue in moments of frustration or anger. You want to be good, respectful, kind—but then you let your words loose, and before you know it, you've done damage that you can't easily undo. That's why James tells us that no one can tame the tongue. On our own, it's impossible. But when we yield our tongues to the Holy Ghost, something miraculous happens.

The Holy Ghost has the power to tame what we cannot. When your tongue is submitted to the Spirit, the rest of your life begins to follow suit. Proverbs 18:21 says, "Death and life are in the power of the tongue." When the Holy Ghost has control of your tongue, you'll find that it begins to speak words of life, not death. You'll speak blessings instead of curses, encouragement instead of discouragement. And when the Spirit is in control of your tongue, your entire body comes into submission to God's will.

THE ULTIMATE YIELDING: SPEAKING IN TONGUES

The ultimate act of yielding your tongue to God is when you allow His Spirit to fill you, and you let Him give utterance through you. There's something incredibly powerful about this kind of surrender. We can praise God in our own native languages—whether it's English, Spanish, or any other language. Even right now, as you read this, you can lift your voice and say, "God, You are worthy to be praised. I love You. I worship Your holy name." And as you do, you can feel the Spirit of God begin to move, because He inhabits the praises of His people. But as powerful as that is, it's still limited by our own understanding.

Here's the reality: God is so much greater than any words we could ever use to describe Him. We might call Him "awesome," but He's far more awesome than our human minds can comprehend. We might say He's "wonderful," but His wonder surpasses anything we can articulate. When we speak in tongues, it's a sign that we've yielded to the Spirit so completely that we are no longer bound by the limitations of our own language. The Holy Ghost begins to speak through us, giving utterance to praise that we couldn't express on our own.

I've experienced moments where I was praising God in ways I couldn't even understand. I didn't know exactly what I was saying, but I could feel His presence all around me—like a fire engulfing me, like a wind blowing through my soul. It's a powerful, humbling experience to be so fully yielded to the Spirit that He begins to praise God through you. When you reach that place of surrender, you know beyond a shadow of a doubt that you are not quenching the Spirit, but yielding to it completely.

THE POWER OF NEW TONGUES

What's even more powerful is that the Holy Ghost doesn't just give us other tongues—languages we don't understand—it also gives us new tongues. These are words we do understand, but they are words we've never spoken before.

Before I fully yielded to the Spirit, my tongue was full of negativity and defeat. I would say things like, "God can't do that for me. I'll always be broken. I'll never be free from the pain of my past. I'll never be more than the labels people have placed on me." Those were the words of my old tongue, the tongue of a man weighed down by sin and shame. But when I allowed the blamelessness of Jesus Christ to replace my brokenness, when I became a new creation in Him, my words began to change.

2 Corinthians 5:17 tells us, "Therefore if any man be in Christ, he is a new creature: old things are passed away; behold, all things are become new." When I became a new creature in Christ, I began to speak with new tongues. Instead of speaking defeat, I began to speak victory. Instead of dwelling on the lies of the enemy, I began to declare the truth of God's Word over my life. My new tongue says things like, "My God is alive, and He is alive in me. He is working in my life. He has set me free. I am no longer depressed because the joy of the Lord is my strength. I am not defeated because God is giving me victory, time and time again. I will live and not die. Everything is going to be alright."

These are the new tongues that the Holy Ghost gives us. They are words of life, words of hope, words of faith. And as you yield to the Spirit, these new tongues will begin to flow naturally. You'll find yourself speaking God's truth, even in the face of difficult circumstances. The more you speak His Word, the more your life will come into alignment with His promises.

THE WELL WITHIN YOU

Jesus also spoke of the Spirit in terms of water—specifically, living water. In John 4:13-14, Jesus told the woman at the well: "Whosoever drinketh of this water shall thirst again: But whosoever drinketh of the water that I shall give him shall never thirst; but the water that I shall give him shall be in him a well of water springing up into everlasting life."

Jesus wasn't saying that we would never feel physical thirst again. He was pointing out that, once we have the Holy Ghost, we don't need to go back to the old wells we used to rely on. Before Christ, we turned to all kinds of wells in an attempt to quench our spiritual thirst. Maybe it was the well of alcohol, drugs, relationships, or even career success. But those wells never fully satisfied the deep thirst in our souls.

When we come to Jesus, we receive a well of living water that's inside of us. We no longer need to turn to the old, broken wells of the world. Now, the well we need is within us, springing up into everlasting life. This living water, the Holy Ghost, satisfies us in ways nothing else can. But here's the important part: we must not quench that well. We must allow the Spirit to flow freely in our lives, nourishing us and guiding us into everlasting life.

STANDING STILL AND LETTING GOD MOVE

There are times in our walk with God when we face situations that seem impossible. We're standing at our own Red Sea, with nowhere to turn. The obstacles before us look insurmountable, and the enemy is closing in behind us. In those moments, everything in our flesh wants to act—to take matters into our own hands. But the Word of God teaches us that there are times when we need to stand still and let God move.

I'm reminded of the story of Moses and the Israelites as they stood at the edge of the Red Sea. The people were panicking, convinced that they were going to die or be taken back into slavery. Exodus 14:11-14 records their cries: "Because there were no graves in Egypt, hast thou taken us away to die in the wilderness? Is not this the word that we did tell thee in Egypt, saying, Let us alone, that we may serve the Egyptians? For it had been better for us to serve the Egyptians, than that we should die in the wilderness."

Moses, in response, told the people: "Fear ye not, stand still, and see the salvation of the Lord. The Lord shall fight for you, and ye shall hold your peace." This wasn't just a call for physical stillness; it was a call for spiritual trust. The Israelites had no way of knowing how God would deliver them, but they had to trust that He would.

In our own lives, we often face moments where it feels like there's no way forward. But just as Moses told the Israelites, sometimes the best thing we can do is stand still and trust that God is already working on our behalf. While we're standing still, God is moving in ways we can't yet see. He's parting the seas, making a way where there seems to be no way.

FAITH IN THE FACE OF THE IMPOSSIBLE

The story of Moses and the Israelites at the Red Sea is such a profound example of what it means to stand still and trust in God's power, even when everything around you says to panic. Imagine being there with the Israelites, standing on the shore of the Red Sea, with no escape in sight. The Egyptian army is closing in, and the only thing separating you from them is a body of water that seems impossible to cross. It's easy to see why they were afraid, why they were ready to give up and go back to Egypt.

But Moses understood something that the people didn't. He knew that God had a plan, even if it wasn't visible yet. In that moment of fear and uncertainty, Moses didn't offer a step-by-step solution. He didn't outline a detailed escape plan. All he said was, "Fear ye not, stand still, and see the salvation of the Lord."* This is a powerful lesson for us. There are times when we won't see how God is going to work things out, but we must trust that He is already moving on our behalf. Sometimes, the best thing we can do is stand still—hold our peace—and allow God to do what only He can do.

Think about what happened next. God, with an invisible hand, parted the waters of the Red Sea. He made a way where there was no way. The Israelites walked through on dry ground, and when they looked back, the waters had collapsed on their enemies, leaving them completely free from the threat of Egypt. This was a miracle that no one could have predicted, yet it's exactly what God does. He moves in ways that defy human understanding.

This is why, when we're standing in front of our own Red Seas, we must resist the temptation to act in the flesh. It's so natural to want to "fix" the situation ourselves. But as Moses demonstrated, the key to victory is often standing still and letting God move. We may not know how He will do it, but we can trust that He will.

THE BATTLE BETWEEN FLESH AND SPIRIT

One of the greatest challenges we face in our walk with God is the constant battle between our flesh and the Spirit. Our flesh wants control. It wants to take matters into its own hands, especially in difficult situations. But the Bible is clear that the flesh does not have the answers. In fact, if we rely on our flesh, we'll only end up quenching the Spirit and missing out on what God wants to do in our lives.

Look at what happens when we act in the flesh. We become anxious, worried, and restless. We try to solve problems in our own strength, and when things don't go as planned, we feel frustrated and defeated. But the Bible teaches us a different way—a way that requires us to surrender our flesh and trust in the Spirit.

Romans 8:6 says, "For to be carnally minded is death; but to be spiritually minded is life and peace." When we allow our flesh to lead, it brings nothing but frustration and spiritual death. But when we surrender to the Spirit, it brings life and peace. That's why it's so important to quench not the Spirit.

Think about the example of Moses at the Red Sea. He could have easily panicked. He could have tried to lead the people in an escape that was doomed to fail. But instead, he stood still and allowed the Spirit of God to move. And because of that, the Israelites experienced a miraculous deliverance that they could never have accomplished in their own strength.

In our own lives, the same principle applies. When we're faced with impossible situations, we have two choices: we can act in the flesh, or we can stand still and trust in the Spirit. When we choose the latter, we open the door for God to move in ways that go beyond anything we could have imagined.

THE POWER OF GOD'S BREATH

When we talk about the Spirit of God, one of the most beautiful metaphors we see in Scripture is that of breath. From the very beginning, God's breath has been synonymous with life and creation. In Genesis

2:7, we read that God formed man from the dust of the ground and breathed into his nostrils the breath of life, and man became a living soul. It was the breath of God that brought Adam to life, and it is the same breath that sustains us today.

This idea of God's breath being life-giving is seen throughout the Bible. When the Spirit of God moves, it is as if God is breathing new life into whatever He touches. We see this in the story of creation, and we see it again in the story of Ezekiel and the valley of dry bones.

In Ezekiel 37, God shows the prophet a valley full of dry bones and asks him, "Can these bones live?" Ezekiel responds, "O Lord God, thou knowest." Then God commands Ezekiel to prophesy to the bones, saying, "O ye dry bones, hear the word of the Lord." As Ezekiel prophesies, the bones begin to come together, flesh and skin cover them, but there is still no life in them. It is only when God commands Ezekiel to prophesy to the wind—the breath of God—that the bones are filled with life.

Ezekiel 37:9-10 says, "Then said he unto me, Prophesy unto the wind, prophesy, son of man, and say to the wind, Thus saith the Lord God; Come from the four winds, O breath, and breathe upon these slain, that they may live. So I prophesied as he commanded me, and the breath came into them, and they lived, and stood up upon their feet, an exceeding great army."

This story is such a powerful reminder of the life-giving power of the Spirit. Just as God breathed life into Adam, and just as He breathed life into the dry bones in Ezekiel's vision, He is constantly breathing life into us through His Spirit. When we speak the Word of God, we are breathing His life into our situations. When we yield to the Spirit, we are allowing the breath of God to move in us and through us.

SPEAK LIFE

There's something powerful that happens when we speak the Word of God into our lives. It's not just empty words or hopeful declarations—it's speaking life. Hebrews 4:12 tells us that "the word of God is quick, and powerful, and sharper than any two-edged sword." When we speak God's Word, we are releasing His power into our circumstances.

Think about this in practical terms. Have you ever noticed how your words can change the atmosphere? When you speak words of fear, doubt, or negativity, it seems to bring a heaviness into the room. But when you speak words of faith, hope, and truth, it lifts the atmosphere. That's because our words have power, and when we align our words with God's Word, we're speaking His life into our situations.

There's a beautiful illustration of this in Deuteronomy 6:4-7: "Hear, O Israel: The Lord our God is one Lord: And thou shalt love the Lord thy God with all thine heart, and with all thy soul, and with all thy might. And these words, which I command thee this day, shall be in thine heart: And thou shalt teach them diligently unto thy children, and shalt talk of them when thou sittest in thine house, and when thou walkest by the way, and when thou liest down, and when thou risest up."

God was commanding the Israelites to speak His Word in every part of their lives. They were to teach it to their children, talk about it as they went about their day, and even write it on the walls of their homes. Why? Because the Word of God is life. When we fill our hearts and minds with His Word, it begins to transform us from the inside out. When we speak His Word over our families, our homes, our finances, and our situations, we are speaking life into those areas.

So, don't be afraid to declare the Word of God over your life. Speak it boldly, with faith, knowing that you are releasing the breath of God into your circumstances. Whether you're facing financial struggles, health issues, or relational challenges, the Word of God has the power to bring life and transformation. Speak it, believe it, and watch God move.

CHAPTER 6

EMBRACE THE WORD

THE POWER OF THE PROPHETIC WORD

In your quest to become blameless before God and abstain from every appearance of evil, one of your closest allies is the power of the prophetic word. Prophecy carries immense power. We see its influence in the Old Testament, in the New Testament, and even in our own lives. The power of prophecy often comes at pivotal moments, speaking directly into our spirits and giving us fresh perspective. This is essential because, as you and I know, our bodies are often at war with us, undermining the work of the Holy Spirit.

A person may resolve to live for the Lord and pursue the good things of God, yet just a short period without prayer, without reading and applying His Word, and without worship can lead to a noticeable spiritual decline. The body begins to backslide, pulling the spirit into a downward spiral. Sometimes, we may not even realize it has happened until we find ourselves snapping at someone or until an old carnal desire surfaces unexpectedly. You may think, "Wait a minute, I thought I already dealt with that." And you likely did. But because our bodies, minds, and hearts are fallen and in the process of dying, we must renew our minds daily to avoid being conformed to this world.

RENEWING AND TRANSFORMATION

Paul addresses this very struggle when he writes in Romans 12:1-2, "I beseech you therefore, brethren, by the mercies of God, that ye present your bodies a living sacrifice, holy, acceptable unto God, which is your reasonable service. And be not conformed to this world: but be ye transformed by the renewing of your mind, that ye may prove what is that good, and acceptable, and perfect, will of God."

There are two critical truths we must grasp from Paul's message. First, if you commit to renewing your mind in the things of God, transformation will follow naturally. Renew your mind in the message of Calvary, in the cleansing power of His blood, in His Word, and in the peace that surpasses all understanding. Let it be renewed in the perfect love that casts out all fear, in the powers of the world to come, and in the work of the Holy Spirit. When you do this, transformation occurs.

However, if you fail to renew your mind, you will inevitably conform to the ways of the world. If you truly wish to backslide, it's simple: stop renewing your mind in the presence of God. Stop receiving His prophetic Word. Stop exposing yourself to His presence. If you are determined to fall away, the path is clear: remove from your life the very powers that convert your soul.

But as for me, I choose to align myself with the believers described in Hebrews 10:39: "But we are not of them who draw back unto perdition; but of them that believe to the saving of the soul."

We should approach the renewing of our minds not as a chore, ritual, or mundane obligation, but as a daily opportunity to draw closer to God and be transformed into His likeness. If you're searching for an example of transformative power, you won't find it in this fallen world. True transformation is found in the church. You won't find anyone in the world, those who worship the gods of this world, who exemplify what you want to become spiritually. No one in this world should hold that place in your life. There is only one who qualifies: Jesus Christ.

1 John 3:2 says it clearly: "Beloved, now are we the sons of God, and it doth not yet appear what we shall be: but we know that, when he shall appear, we shall be like him; for we shall see him as he is."

As for me, I want to be like Jesus. I want to stand blameless before the Lord. I long for the innocence of Christ to come upon my life. But I cannot accomplish this on my own. I need God's help, and I need to search and obey the scriptures. I must rejoice always, pray without ceasing, give thanks in all things, and never quench the Spirit of God. I must not despise prophecy.

2 Peter 1:20-21 affirms this: "Knowing this first, that no prophecy of the scripture is of any private interpretation. For the prophecy came not in old time by the will of man: but holy men of God spake as they were moved by the Holy Ghost."

THE CONSISTENCY AND POWER OF GOD'S WORD

God's inspired Word is not hidden; it's all here, open to us. Just as Isaiah spoke impossible things that eventually came to pass, we too must trust that the Word of God, spoken through prophecy, will be fulfilled in our own lives. You can look at any body of writings across various fields or industries, compare one era to another, and you'll often find dramatic changes in perspective. What was once considered expert knowledge might be disqualified a decade or centuries later as new information is discovered. But when you look at the Word of the Lord, you're looking at writings that span millennia, yet remain consistent. That's powerful.

The writers of Scripture came from vastly different backgrounds—shepherds, lawyers, doctors, gardeners, and tree dressers—yet they all shared one commonality: they were alone with God in a secret place. When they spoke, it wasn't their own will or desires they expressed. They spoke the anointed Word of God as the Holy Spirit moved upon them.

In Isaiah 51, God says, "I have put my words in thy mouth." It's noteworthy that He says He put His words in their mouths, not their minds. We might expect God to first place His word in their minds before it came from their mouths, but sometimes He bypasses our minds altogether to prevent us from corrupting His message with our unbelief. If God told you to stand up and proclaim, "A virgin shall conceive and bring forth a son," you better be certain you heard from God. Sometimes, God bypasses the mind and places His word directly in the mouth.

Isaiah 7:14 says, "Therefore the Lord himself shall give you a sign; Behold, a virgin shall conceive, and bear a son, and shall call his name Immanuel." Isaiah 9:6-7 declares, "For unto us a child is born, unto us a son is given: and the government shall be upon his shoulder: and his name shall be called Wonderful, Counsellor, The mighty God, The everlasting Father, The Prince of Peace. Of the increase of his government and peace there shall be no end, upon the throne of David, and upon his kingdom, to order it, and to establish it with judgment and with justice from henceforth even forever. The zeal of the Lord of hosts will perform this." Isaiah 53:2 adds, "For he shall grow up before him as a tender plant, and as a root out of a dry ground..."

When the prophet Isaiah delivered the word of the Lord, much of what he said made no sense at the time. These passages describe what seemed to be impossible events. He spoke of water flowing in the desert, of rivers and streams in dry places, and of pools forming in parched ground. The idea of a virgin giving birth to a child was, by human standards, an impossibility. Isaiah was speaking things that were not as though they were—he was delivering the word of prophecy.

Just as Isaiah did not see these things fulfilled in his lifetime, we may not always see immediate results from the Word spoken over us. He simply spoke the word, believed it, and left it up to the people to decide whether they would believe as well. No matter how impossible the word may seem, you can always trust in the word of God. It is more reliable than any newspaper, journal, or writing by any individual. The word of God stands above all else.

Psalm 138:2 affirms this, "...for thou hast magnified thy word above all thy name." If you are a true Christian, then you are part of the people of the Name. We believe in the power of the name of Jesus. We are baptized in His name, for there is no other name under heaven given among men by which we must be saved. In the name of Jesus, we receive healing and protection. We emphatically declare that whatever we do in word or deed, we do in the name of Jesus Christ.

Mark 16:17-18 echoes this truth, "And these signs shall follow them that believe; In my name shall they cast out devils; they shall speak with new tongues; they shall take up serpents; and if they drink any deadly thing, it shall not hurt them; they shall lay hands on the sick, and they shall recover."

These signs are a testament to the power and authority we carry in His name—authority we receive when we fully embrace His prophetic Word. As the psalmist declares, "The name of the Lord is a strong tower: the righteous run into it and are safe."

While we exalt the name of Jesus for the power it holds, when we speak of the word of God, we are speaking of something the Lord has magnified even beyond His own name. The word of God is the ultimate, all-powerful force.

The word of God has the power to bring order to chaos. It can look upon an earth that is formless, empty, and covered in darkness, and by His spoken word, it can bring forth light and life. God's creative power is manifest through His word. When we speak of prophecy, we are speaking of something that contains life—there is life in the prophetic utterance of God's word.

Did you know that when a preacher stands behind the pulpit, he is prophesying? This is the gift of prophecy—forth-telling. It's not just about predicting things like which tooth will get a cavity in two weeks; that would fall under the gift of the word of knowledge. The word of knowledge reveals something beneficial and edifying that a person would have no natural way of knowing. People can operate in this gift, but they must be cautious and ensure they are absolutely in the Spirit when using the gifts of the Spirit.

The gift of prophecy, however, is the declaration of the word of the Lord. It's speaking His holy word, proclaiming the truth of the gospel of Jesus Christ. That's why I take great pleasure in being a preacher of the gospel. I know that His word is going forth and accomplishing exactly what He has purposed.

But the power is not in me; it's in the word. It's not even in how I deliver it. I pray that the Lord will anoint my delivery, my tongue, and the structure of my message, but all of that pales in comparison to the true power of God's word.

TRUST IN GOD'S WORD

In my own ministry, I've experienced firsthand the power of the Word, even when it doesn't seem to connect immediately. A sermon can be clumsy in structure and still possess the power to save a human soul. It may be delivered in a way that lacks human effectiveness, but it can still reach into the hearts of men, women, boys, and girls, turning their spirits toward God. That's the power of prophecy—it's the declaration of God's word.

This is incredibly sacred to me. I don't believe in preaching anything just because it appeals to me. I believe in preaching and teaching the Word of God. I don't believe in manipulating scripture through mishandling it. I believe in rightly dividing the word of truth so that people can be edified by the power of Almighty God. When we rightly divide the word, the church multiplies. But if we add to or subtract from it, the church is divided. We neither add nor subtract—we preach the true word of God.

This isn't just for the pulpit or those called to preaching ministry. Every child of God is called to preach the word. When storms come, preach the word. When the floodwaters rise, preach the word. When the enemy comes in like a flood, preach the word. When the adversary sets himself against us, we preach the word. We live preaching it, and we die preaching it.

This is the power of the word: when the grass withers and the flowers fade, the word of God will stand forever. Heaven and earth will pass away, but God's word will never pass away. Take a long look at the things around you—drive through the countryside, visit the mountains, walk along the beach, explore the rivers, the lakes, and the cities—because all of it will pass away. Enjoy the beauty of creation, but in all your getting, get a revelation of what will stand forever. Cherish what will outlast heaven and earth.

If something has a beginning, it will also have an end. But not God's word. Men have tried to ban it and burn it, but the word of God is still here, and we are still declaring it. The Jewish people had no nation, no place to preserve their sacred texts, yet it didn't matter. The word of God is forever settled in heaven. It's recorded in the most enduring place of all: eternity.

This is the power of God's prophecy to man, and it is not to be despised. It should be cherished and celebrated. Prophets have long been despised by the world. When you commit to speaking the word of God, you take on a heavy task. You also take on the same bullseye Jesus carried. When you declare, "Thus saith the Lord," get ready for a target on your life. The devil hates you, and those whom he persuades will hate you as well. But none of that matters—just preach the word of God.

If you are living for the Lord, keep living for Him, but understand this: the devil hates you and desires to sift you as wheat. You and I have an adversary, and he will use whatever tactic he can to trip you up and mock you. He is cruel beyond measure. He will tempt you, enticing you with the allure of pleasure, and the moment you fall into that temptation, he will swallow you whole and mock you relentlessly. He mocks us all the way into our downfall.

If you do manage to get past a fall by the help of God, Satan will return in various seasons to tempt you again and remind you of where you stumbled. You'll never truly know if you've repented of a particular sin until the devil tempts you with it once more. If you've truly repented and turned away from that sin, you'll know by your response when the enemy tries to lure you again. For example, if pornography was once a temptation and you repented of it, leaving it behind with God's help, you'll know you've truly overcome it when the devil uses it again to try and stop your walk with God.

The Bible instructs us to remember where we have fallen. Let the Holy Spirit quicken and check your spirit so that you can resist the devil, submit to God, and watch the devil flee. It is the prophetic word of God that will deliver you from evil and lead you away from temptation. The preaching and teaching of God's word, when hidden in your heart, will prick your conscience, convict your spirit, renew your mind, transform your life, and save you from sin.

I can stand as a testimony to this truth. If it weren't for the preaching and teaching of God's word, I wouldn't be here today. Maybe you, too, were set on a particular path, convinced it was the right direction. Perhaps you found yourself in a valley of decision—depressed, oppressed, downtrodden, or discouraged. Maybe you struggled with the same sin for years, trying to break free. It was hearing the preaching of the word that made the difference. Somewhere, in a secret place, the preacher touched the throne of God and came away with a word just for you.

I don't know a preacher who enjoys delivering a bad sermon. I'm one of them, and I beat myself up when I feel like I've preached a bad sermon. I've said things like, "That didn't go over like I thought," or, "That made as much sense as a soup sandwich." I do this because I know how few opportunities I have to reach people's hearts, and I don't want to waste even one. Every time the word goes forth, it takes on a life of its own and ministers to each person differently. I've learned that when I think I've preached badly, it's often just my own fleshly misunderstanding.

I remember one Sunday morning when I preached a message that wasn't typical for a Sunday. I felt uncomfortable preaching it. Afterward, I was convinced I had missed the will of God by a mile. The response was nonexistent, and I went back to my office disappointed. But then, the elder pastor of the church came in and sat across from me. With tears in his eyes, he said, "As long as the Lord allows it, preach that message everywhere you go. We need that kind of preaching. Thank you for obeying the Holy Ghost. Don't worry about their response. Give the word of God time to settle into their hearts."

By the time we gathered again that evening, we witnessed a mighty move of the Holy Ghost. Several people received the Holy Ghost and were renewed by His Spirit. People testified of depression lifting, and some who were ready to give up on their faith rejoiced that God had spoken to them. Among those filled with the Spirit was an eighty-nine-year-old devout Catholic woman who received the gift of the Holy Ghost, speaking in tongues.

I had to repent for how I felt after preaching that message. What if everything had gone the way I wanted? I was expecting the altars to be filled, people to lay down their vices, and confessions to pour out. But God was saying, "Let my word do what it does. Someone's heart is being prepared. All they needed was the pure, simple, and powerful word." If we could just learn to trust God's word and let Him be God, He would trust us with His glory and power.

PERSECUTION CAN BE A BLESSING?

Matthew 5:10-16 says, "Blessed are they which are persecuted for righteousness' sake: for theirs is the kingdom of heaven. Blessed are ye when men shall revile you and persecute you and shall say all manner of evil against you falsely, for my sake. Rejoice and be exceedingly glad, for great is your reward in heaven: for so persecuted they the prophets which were before you. Ye are the salt of the earth, but if the salt have lost its savour, wherewith shall it be salted? It is thenceforth good for nothing but to be cast out and trodden underfoot of men. Ye are the light of the world. A city that is set on a hill cannot be hid. Neither do men light a candle and put it under a bushel, but on a candlestick, and it giveth light unto all that are in the house. Let your light so shine before men, that they may see your good works and glorify your Father which is in heaven."

Did you catch what Jesus said? He didn't say, "Blessed are you when you get a new BMW and a 7,000-square-foot house." He said, "Blessed are ye when men revile you and persecute you." God's way of counting blessings is different from the world's. Here's the opportunity we have—an opportunity that only comes when we are reviled and persecuted. You have the chance to be the salt of the earth when you are reviled. You have the chance to be the light of the world when you are persecuted. You have the chance to let your light shine before men, with no bushel covering it, when people say all manner of evil against you falsely, for the Lord's sake.

CHAPTER 7

PROVE IT!

Proving all things is incredibly important, especially when it comes to a sensitive topic for some—the discerning of spirits. This is a vital part of your walk with God. The Bible tells us that it's important for God's people to be taught the difference between the holy and the profane. We live in a time when many preachers avoid clarifying that certain things in this world are profane. They shy away from teaching the difference between what is holy and what is profane. As a result, you and I have a responsibility—especially with the Holy Spirit as our guide—to learn what is right and wrong and to obey what God is revealing to us. When the Holy Spirit throws up a red flag, don't ignore it.

NAVIGATE WITH THE SPIRIT

Too often, we trample over what the Holy Spirit is trying to tell us. We get involved in something we know we shouldn't be, and in doing so, we override the work of the Spirit in our lives. This eventually leads to quenching the Spirit.

It's important not to confuse the work of the preacher with the work of the Holy Spirit. The preacher's role is to preach the gospel of Jesus Christ. As 2 Timothy 4:2 says, "Preach the word; be instant in season, out of season; reprove, rebuke, exhort with all longsuffering and doctrine." The work of the preacher—and really every saint of God—is to, "Study to shew thyself approved unto God, a workman that needeth not to be ashamed, rightly dividing the word of truth" (2 Timothy 2:15).

When it comes to making the right decisions, you alone are accountable for your actions. No one can do the right thing for you. Take responsibility for what you do, whether it's good or bad, and understand that God has placed His word and will in your hands for you to act upon. This can be daunting, especially when you consider how deceptive and evil the human heart is, and how your flesh is often in league with the enemy of your soul. Life is full of temptations, so you can't trust your heart because it lies frequently. You can't trust your flesh because it wars against your soul and is, in reality, an enemy of the Spirit of God.

Proverbs 16:25 says, "There is a way that seemeth right unto a man, but the end thereof are the ways of death." I can relate to that, as I have zero navigational skills. My wife, on the other hand, doesn't even have to know the area well, and she can still figure out where we're supposed to be going with ease. I remember early in our marriage, I'd say things like, "I think I know where I'm at," and she'd respond, "If you know so much, you should have driven." Needless to say, I don't say that anymore! Thank God for GPS. Even with GPS, I still get distracted and have to turn around multiple times because I get confused. When she's driving, I just go along for the ride because she has a great sense of direction, something I lack entirely. Over time, I've learned that if I feel like I should turn left, I should probably turn right. If I think I should keep going straight, I might need to make a U-turn because I most likely passed the destination. And if I think I've passed it, I probably haven't gone far enough yet.

This, of course, is a silly little analogy, and I wish it weren't my reality, but alas, it is what it is. However, over time, you learn that your flesh cannot be trusted. It's interesting to think about the will of the flesh because it has its own desires and preferences. It has its own tendencies, and these desires and preferences almost always lean toward what is convenient and advantageous to us. Ironically, it often ends up benefiting us the most. While that isn't necessarily wrong or bad, it can often mean the difference between staying blameless or falling into temptation and sin—something we should obviously want to avoid.

In your life of serving and waiting on the Lord, you will hopefully come to learn that "the first shall be last, and the last shall be first" and that "it is more blessed to give than to receive." You must let the Holy Spirit guide and teach you, and through that process, you will learn how to prove all things.

THE SUBTLE DANGER OF MISLEADING SPIRITS

We must also understand that many deceptive spirits will rise up to try and tempt us, leading us toward something that is incorrect and invalid. In Matthew 6, when the disciples asked Jesus to teach them how to pray, He gave them what we now call "The Lord's Prayer." However, this prayer is really for everyone—it's what we should all pray.

In Matthew 6:9-13, Jesus says, "After this manner therefore pray ye: Our Father which art in heaven, Hallowed be thy name. Thy kingdom come. Thy will be done in earth, as it is in heaven. Give us this day our daily bread." This is interesting because it reveals the point at which Jesus recommends we begin praying—at the start of the day. He's telling us to begin each day with prayer. "Give us this day our daily bread." The day is just beginning, and we are asking God to provide us with what He desires for us that day—nothing more, nothing less. In Matthew 6:12-13, Jesus continues, "And forgive us our debts, as we forgive our debtors. And lead us not into temptation, but deliver us from evil: For thine is the kingdom, and the power, and the glory, for ever. Amen."

Before we do anything else—in order to prove all things, to discern the spirits, to practice wisdom, and to have understanding about the right decisions and the right direction to go in—we must first and foremost pray to God for deliverance from evil. We need God to protect us from making wrong decisions. This shows how little I trust myself to make the right choices. I have to pray that Jesus will deliver me from evil, deliver me from pride, and prevent pride from influencing my decisions. I need deliverance from greed. I want the Lord to deliver me from the lust of my eyes and the lust of my flesh. We don't want these temptations to influence the choices we are going to make.

If I am carnal, not seeking God, and not praying, I can easily confuse a lust of my flesh for a desire of the Spirit. We really need to understand this because so few realize how serious it truly is. If you're not praying and seeking God, it's very easy to confuse the lusts of your flesh for spiritual desires. This leads to wrong decisions and ultimately puts you face-to-face with evil. That's when you end up dealing with the appearance of evil.

If you'll prove all things and hold fast to that which is good, with the help of the Holy Spirit, you won't have to worry about succumbing to the appearance of evil. That's what I want. That's what the apostle Paul wanted. That's what the Lord Jesus Christ wants. It's my desire to equip people to abstain from all appearance of evil. You don't just haphazardly walk up to evil and say, "I am a child of God. What's your name?" No. Evil won't be honest. Evil won't tell you, "I am evil. This is how you recognize me for what I am." Evil will disguise itself as anything but evil. It will take on any good quality you can imagine, hiding its true nature. It will never be honest with you because it is evil. Don't depend on your flesh. Don't depend on your heart. Don't depend on the evil thing or the evil person to reveal their true nature.

THE GIFT OF DISCERNMENT

You need to have discerning power. Read this carefully: discerning spirits is a gift of the Spirit. The Spirit of God gives us the ability to discern spirits. You don't have to be some super prophet to discern spirits. You don't have to be Elijah, Elisha, Isaiah, or John the Baptist. What you need is to be filled with and remain full of the Holy Spirit. There are people who don't have the Holy Spirit but have somehow tapped into the "gift of suspicion." They get it wrong most of the time, but sometimes they get it right. Let me be clear—that's not discernment; it's something bestowed upon us by us. We end up prejudging, unfairly labeling others, and holding people accountable for what others have done to us. We paint with broad strokes when dealing with people's humanity. Instead, we must love without suspicion and allow the Holy Spirit within us to prove all things and hold fast to what is good.

To prove all things, the first step is to pray that the Lord would lead you not into temptation and deliver you from evil. We desperately need God to get involved in the decision-making infrastructure of our lives. The apparatus that guides my decisions needs the voice of the Counselor to make wise and good choices. Pray specific prayers. Ask God to take away wicked desires and replace them with godly ones. Pray that God would give you the feelings you ought to have.

There are many people who live their lives condemned by their feelings. They feel a certain way about a situation, and they beat themselves up because they know they shouldn't feel that way. They feel one way about a person but know the Lord doesn't feel that way, so they torment themselves in their minds. In reality, it's an unclean spirit whispering in their ears, manipulating their thoughts and emotions, trying to make them feel a certain way. This is what the apostle Paul meant when he warned us not to be ignorant of Satan's devices. He has devices, and if you're not proving all things, you will fall prey to them. It's knowledge, wisdom, and understanding of the things of God that help us prove all things and walk confidently in the Holy Spirit.

When a foreign feeling enters your emotional makeup, and it feels real and genuine, but you've been praying in the Spirit and you know in your heart of hearts that you're not supposed to feel that way, take a moment. Bounce what you're hearing and feeling off the Word of God, and you'll recognize that it's not from Him. You need to believe that you are a blood-bought, Spirit-filled, sanctified, and justified child of God.

When people don't understand the devil's devices, they often succumb to their feelings. They may not recognize their patterns of thinking but assume, "Because I feel this way, this must be who I am. This defines me. I must act on this feeling because it's who I am anyway." But the purpose of being saved from this untoward generation is so that you don't act upon ungodly feelings, desires, or impulses. You've been set free from those ungodly impulses. This is not who you are. This does not define you. You have been filled with the Holy Spirit, and you have been washed in the blood of the Lamb. And understand this: if you haven't been filled with the Holy Spirit, God can fill you with His Spirit at any time. The promise is to you and to your children.

The enemy of your soul knows that you are flesh and blood, so he operates on a different spiritual plane than you do throughout your day and week. He will speak into your life on a different frequency, one you may not expect. You won't often hear an audible voice. It will come as a feeling. If you don't recognize that it's him, you begin to get depressed. You start looking down on yourself and others. He will condemn you, label you, and beat you down. Sometimes, he'll whisper in your ear about other people. Suddenly, you're looking at someone and thinking you're discerning something, but you're really not. What you're doing is heading down a path that could hurt someone or damage a relationship. This is why it's so important to prove all things, so those ungodly feelings and impulses don't take root in your life and you can abstain from all appearance of evil.

1 John 4:1-4 says, "Beloved, believe not every spirit, but try the spirits whether they are of God: because many false prophets are gone out into the world. Hereby know ye the Spirit of God: Every spirit that confesseth that Jesus Christ is come in the flesh is of God: And every spirit that confesseth not that Jesus Christ is come in the flesh is not of God: and this is that spirit of antichrist, whereof ye have heard that it should come; and even now already is it in the world. Ye are of God, little children, and have overcome them: because greater is he that is in you, than he that is in the world."

When we speak of Jesus Christ coming in the flesh, we're speaking of Jehovah salvation, the anointed Messiah, coming in the flesh. It's important to understand what we're saying here. Jehovah is my salvation, and the Anointed One—the Messiah—has come in the flesh, and His name is Jesus Christ. If a spirit does not agree with this, it is not of God. This is why you should avoid filling your mind with songs and messages from people who don't believe in *Jehovah salvation*, the anointed Messiah, coming in the flesh. These voices are speaking and singing from the vantage point of the antichrist. This is also why we don't follow the teachings of anyone who denies that Jehovah salvation—the Messiah—has come in the flesh, because they come from the spirit of the antichrist.

We don't follow their social media platforms. We don't repost their videos. It's the spirit of antichrist. Many people imagine the antichrist as some terrifying beast rising out of the ground with multiple heads, covered in horns and scales, with big red eyes, a pitchfork, a pointed tail, and breathing fire. They think, "I've never seen anything like that, so the antichrist must be something else." In reality, the spirit of the antichrist comes in much subtler forms, often through false religion. Let's not forget how Jesus was crucified—He was crucified because of religious objection to what He was doing. This is the epitome of the spirit of antichrist.

"Believe not every spirit." Unfortunately, this command often goes over people's heads. Many think, "I've never had a spirit talk to me," but that's simply not true. You've had multiple spirits speak to you since the day began. If you understood how much activity goes on in the spirit world, you wouldn't be as afraid. Someone once said to me, "I feel a bad spirit." Of course, they did. Unclean and evil spirits are all over the place. I'm not belittling anyone for that statement, but we must understand that these spirits are active at all times. Know this: we are not overcome by them. The Word of God says that we have overcome them because greater is He that is in us than he that is in the world. We don't need to be intimidated by the idea of being overcome. We don't entertain the thought of being defeated. We have authority over it in the name of Jesus Christ.

I hope this doesn't come across as arrogant, but I've lived for God long enough to recognize how the devil operates. I remember clearly one year during Thanksgiving week, I was sitting with my family in my in-laws' living room when a strange feeling began to creep up on me. It was familiar, but I couldn't quite place it. There had been a time when I was so down on myself—discouraged, beating myself up emotionally. Let's be honest, it's hard to escape yourself sometimes. I was feeling low, anxious, intimidated, and overwhelmed by pressure, and it was causing fear and terror. This was a spiritual battle threatening to consume me.

I looked over at my wife and asked her to excuse me so I could go to the church and pray. When she asked why, I simply told her, "I just have a bad feeling." I knew deep down that how I was feeling was not from God. I prayed for understanding, asking the Lord to help me make sense of what I was experiencing. In my heart, I knew I wasn't supposed to feel this way. As I prayed, the Lord began to speak into my spirit—not an audible voice, but revelation. The feeling I was having was coming from an unclean spirit whispering into my life, and the Lord showed me why I was feeling that way. It was as if I was being given a glimpse into how Satan views me.

The Lord was allowing me to feel what hell was shouting at me so I could better understand how to combat it. The answer is always to turn to Him. When you don't understand a feeling or emotion, turn to God. The way I felt in that moment was not from Him, and it had no place in my life. Because it wasn't from God, I knew I didn't need to dwell on it. Thank God, the devil is still a liar! If it's coming from the devil, it's a lie. If the devil says you're defeated, it's a lie. If he says you won't have victory, it's a lie. If the devil stirs up a feeling or emotion within you, that feeling and emotion cannot be trusted. If the devil says you can't experience what the Lord has for you, it's a lie. The truth is the opposite—you will have victory. You will win. You can experience what God has for you. Let God be true, and every man and every devil a liar.

Philippians 4:8 is perhaps one of the best places to understand how to prove all things and hold fast to that which is good, "Finally, brethren, whatsoever things are true, whatsoever things are honest, whatsoever things are just, whatsoever things are pure, whatsoever things are lovely, whatsoever things are of good report; if there be any virtue, and if there be any praise, think on these things."

Don't let your mind wander aimlessly. Some people let their minds "wonder" until they end up "wandering." It sounds like this: "Well, I was just wondering…" and after wondering for so long, you start wandering. We need to be able to prove the thoughts that enter our minds. Don't feed your mind with thoughts that are anti-God, anti-Christ, anti-church, anti-faith, or anti-Bible. Don't fill your mind with thoughts that are trying to tear down what God has built up inside of you.

Read this carefully: You have the blessing of the Lord upon your life. Your eyes and your ears are windows to your soul. Don't allow those windows to be infiltrated by spirits or words that are not of God. Think on things that are lovely. Think on things that are true. Think on things that are of good report. Paul was helping us understand how to prove all things. Don't think on things that are dishonest.

Don't think on things that are impure. Don't think on things that are of a bad report. When someone brings you a bad report, do you know what to do with it? The answer isn't to text it to someone or share it vaguely on social media. Instead, take that bad report to God in prayer. Yes, there's a lot of negativity in the world, but bring it to God in prayer.

As I'm writing this, I can already feel in the Spirit that some people will question, "What if I can't discipline my thoughts? What if I don't want to think about something, but I do? I'm just not strong enough to filter my thoughts and guard my mind." You're absolutely right—you're not strong enough. Neither am I. We don't have enough willpower. Bring it to God in prayer and let the Holy Spirit filter it. Let the helmet of salvation, which guards your mind, slip over you and protect your thoughts. When you pray, tell the Lord, "My desire is to think what you want me to think." In time, your mind will become more fixed on the good things of God. The more distance you put between yourself and exposure to negative or harmful thoughts, the more disciplined your mind will become.

Don't become overconfident. Don't think of yourself as something when you are nothing. We need God's help with this. Fill your mind with thoughts of praise, truth, things that are lovely, virtuous, pure, just, and of good report. Think on His word. Think on His Spirit. I want to emphasize this: the more distance and time you place between yourself and those negative influences, the more disciplined your mind will become.

God will help you do this. Invite Him to help, and then yield to His help. If a thought enters your mind that shouldn't be there, call on the name of Jesus immediately. Don't let it linger. If it returns, pray again. If it resurfaces as you're lying awake at night, don't mull it over and revisit it in the morning. Give it to the Lord and rest, knowing that He's keeping your mind. Before you know it, you'll become more disciplined with each declaration of the name of Jesus, and you'll find yourself praying without ceasing. What better way to spend your time than declaring the name of Jesus? It works with fear. It works with doubt. It works with lust. It works with anxiety. It works to sanctify your mind completely. The result is that you will have a disciplined thought life, you'll be able to prove all things, and you'll hold fast to that which is good. If there be any virtue, and if there be any praise, think on these things.

I want to emphasize the importance of proving all things. Paul's letter to the Romans provides another great foundation for this concept of living for the Lord. Romans 12:1 says, "I beseech you therefore, brethren, by the mercies of God, that ye present your bodies a living sacrifice, holy, acceptable unto God, which is your reasonable service." Hear, O Church of the Living God, the command of the Lord: Present your bodies as a living sacrifice. Do not seek to fulfill the lust of your flesh, the lust of the eyes, or the pride of life. Present your bodies as a living sacrifice—holy, acceptable unto God, which is your reasonable service. We're not talking about works of the Law here; we're talking about the reasonable service of a child of God who has been brought out of darkness and into His marvelous light. Present your bodies a living sacrifice, holy, and acceptable unto God, which is your reasonable service.

Romans 12:2 continues, "And be not conformed to this world: but be ye transformed by the renewing of your mind, that ye may prove what is that good, and acceptable, and perfect, will of God." Transformation happens in the mind. It's a transformation of thoughts, ideologies, identity, and nature. It's not just a transformation—it's a renewing of the mind. When you renew your mind, you are renewing it in the work of Calvary. You are renewing your mind with the blood of Jesus Christ. If you hear the phrase, "the blood of Jesus," and your response is, "Meh," you need to have your mind renewed. This is not just another topic; there is power in the blood of Jesus Christ. If you hear about heaven, New Jerusalem, and the promise of living forever, and your reaction is a yawn, you need to have your mind renewed.

This is how transformation occurs—by the renewing of your mind. Someone once said, *"He brought me out of darkness. I was in chains of addiction. I was bound by fear. I was held captive by my failures. But He brought me out of all that anyway."* If that testimony doesn't stir joy in your soul, put clapping in your hands, a song on your lips, and a shout in your spirit, then you need to have your mind renewed.

RENEWING THE MIND: A DAILY NECESSITY

If you will renew your mind in the truth of God's Word, you will be transformed—completely transformed. You will become someone entirely different than who you used to be. I've seen people transformed so completely that even their arresting officers and court officials didn't recognize them when compared to their old mugshots. I remember my first youth leader and teen Sunday school teacher, David. He was once a scary man, filled with hate. But when God got a hold of him and took that hate out of his heart, it led to a total transformation. He cleaned himself up, even shaved his massive black beard. He had once sat in the back pew glaring at people from behind that beard. After his transformation by the Holy Spirit, people could barely recognize him in a photograph. That's what happens when you're not conformed to this world but are transformed by the renewing of your mind.

When you rehearse the fact that Jesus paid it all, when you remind yourself that all to Him you owe, and when you cling to the truth that nothing but the blood of Jesus saves you, it keeps you from being conformed to this world. My plan every morning is to renew my mind. When I wake up, I'll take a moment to give thanks, count my blessings, praise and worship Him, and open His Word to read scriptures I've read many times before. Why? Because I need to be renewed by the transforming of my mind. I don't want anything to do with the old Dylan—the fearful, lustful, prideful, arrogant, ignorant, and rebellious Dylan. I want Jesus to transform my whole being—body, soul, and spirit.

If you don't renew your mind, you'll start fearing what the carnal mind fears. You'll begin worshipping what the carnal mind worships. You'll crave what the carnal mind craves. You'll start treating people the way the world treats them, and you'll view others the way the carnal world does. But if you renew your mind, you'll be transformed to Him, not conformed to them.

Notice what Romans 12:2 says: "... that ye may prove what is that good, and acceptable, and perfect, will of God." There are things that are simply not acceptable to God. I pray that none of those things are found in or on His children. I don't want anything unacceptable to Him to be present in my life. I'm not so foolish as to think I know what all those things are, but if I renew my mind daily, I will have discernment—even of myself.

When we talk about the discernment of spirits, we must often discern whether what we're sensing is the gift of the Holy Spirit or just the "gift of suspicion"—and I use "gift" facetiously here. We need to know the difference.

The gift of suspicion makes you focus solely on the spirits of people around you. The gift of discerning spirits, however, allows you to see not only the spirits of others but also your own spirit. That's the key difference. With suspicion, you're unable to look at yourself to see what needs correction. You only see what others need to fix. But with the discernment of spirits, you can see your own shortcomings as clearly as you see everyone else's. You'll be able to recognize where you've gone wrong, where your attitude is off, or where your spirit is not right. You'll see how you're not treating people as you should, and the Holy Spirit will convict you. When that happens, it doesn't take a major issue for you to own up to it. You can simply say, "I'm sorry. Please forgive me." When this takes place between two Spirit-filled believers, the response is, "I forgive you." The matter is resolved, and peace follows. But you can't get that with the gift of suspicion.

Why can't we hold grudges or keep people accountable for what they've done to us? Because Jesus paid it all. We're trying to make people pay for something they owe us, but Jesus has already paid it with His precious blood. Someone might say, "You don't understand, they owe me!" I understand that what they did was wrong, but if you truly believe that Jesus paid it all, you need to forgive.

SOLOMON'S WISDOM IN ACTION

1 Kings 3:5-9 tells the story of Solomon's dream, "In Gibeon the LORD appeared to Solomon in a dream by night: and God said, Ask what I shall give thee. And Solomon said, Thou hast shewed unto thy servant David my father great mercy, according as he walked before thee in truth, and in righteousness, and in uprightness of heart with thee; and thou hast kept for him this great kindness, that thou hast

given him a son to sit on his throne, as it is this day. And now, O Lord my God, thou hast made thy servant king instead of David my father: and I am but a little child: I know not how to go out or come in. And thy servant is in the midst of thy people which thou hast chosen, a great people, that cannot be numbered nor counted for multitude. Give therefore thy servant an understanding heart to judge thy people, that I may discern between good and bad: for who is able to judge this thy so great a people?"

All of this transpired in a dream. Solomon was likely in his late teens or early twenties at the time. The foundation of him receiving an answer to this prayer was his humility. He recognized, understood, and admitted that he didn't have what it took to fulfill the great calling God had placed upon him. So he prayed, "Give me an understanding heart that I may judge your people, that I may discern between good and bad." How often should leaders and those in ministry pray this prayer? Every day.

Watch the Lord's response, in 1 Kings 3:10-14, "And the speech pleased the Lord, that Solomon had asked this thing. And God said unto him, Because thou hast asked this thing, and hast not asked for thyself long life; neither hast asked riches for thyself, nor hast asked the life of thine enemies; but hast asked for thyself understanding to discern judgment; Behold, I have done according to thy words: lo, I have given thee a wise and an understanding heart; so that there was none like thee before thee, neither after thee shall any arise like unto thee. And I have also given thee that which thou hast not asked, both riches, and honour: so that there shall not be any among the kings like unto thee all thy days. And if thou wilt walk in my ways, to keep my statutes and my commandments, as thy father David did walk, then I will lengthen thy days."

How many prayers have we prayed that were like this? Whatever you're going through and wherever you are in your life, pray this prayer: "Lord, give me an understanding heart. This is too big for me to handle on my own. I can't do this. Help me to discern properly. Help me to prove all things. Help me to know good from bad and bad from good." This is a prayer that God will answer. You'll be able to prove all things, discern properly, and understand in your heart what is right and what is wrong.

But don't pray this as a stepping stone to what you feel is greater. God knows the thoughts and intents of the heart. Be sincere. Be honest. Pray with humility, and you'll not only see this prayer answered, but God will begin to add to your life things you didn't even ask for.

1 Kings 3:15 says, "And Solomon awoke; and, behold, it was a dream." If Solomon was anything like me, when I'm having a really good dream and wake up in the middle of the night, I hate that the dream ended. I sometimes hope that if I go back to sleep, I'll continue the dream. But that's not what Solomon did.

1 Kings 3:15-22 continues the story, "And Solomon awoke; and, behold, it was a dream. And he came to Jerusalem, and stood before the ark of the covenant of the Lord, and offered up burnt offerings, and offered peace offerings, and made a feast to all his servants. Then came there two women, that were harlots, unto the king, and stood before him. And the one woman said, O my lord, I and this woman dwell in one house; and I was delivered of a child with her in the house. And it came to pass the third day after that I was delivered, that this woman was delivered also: and we were together; there was no stranger with us in the house, save we two in the house. And this woman's child died in the night; because she overlaid it. And she arose at midnight, and took my son from beside me, while thine handmaid

slept, and laid it in her bosom, and laid her dead child in my bosom. And when I rose in the morning to give my child suck, behold, it was dead: but when I had considered it in the morning, behold, it was not my son, which I did bear. And the other woman said, Nay; but the living is my son, and the dead is thy son. And this said, No; but the dead is thy son, and the living is my son. Thus they spake before the king." King Solomon was faced with a dilemma. He had to prove all things. He had to discern between truth and lies.

1 Kings 3:23-24 says, "Then said the king, The one saith, This is my son that liveth, and thy son is the dead: and the other saith, Nay; but thy son is the dead, and my son is the living. And the king said, Bring me a sword." I'm telling you, you've got the only sword you need in your life—the sword of the Spirit, which is the Word of God. There is only one way to settle every dispute: bring me a sword. It doesn't matter how convincing the argument may seem. *Bring me the sword of the Spirit,* which is the Word of God.

1 Kings 3:25 continues, "And the king said, Divide the living child in two, and give half to the one, and half to the other." Solomon was just nineteen years old. The people standing by were probably thinking, "What kind of lunatic is on the throne? He's talking about cutting a baby in two! All we needed was a simple answer about who's telling the truth, and he's suggesting this crazy solution. He's lost it!" But they didn't know that God had given Solomon a discerning heart and the wisdom to prove all things. He was using that wisdom to discern the lie from the truth.

1 Kings 3:26-27 says, "Then spake the woman whose the living child was unto the king, for her bowels yearned upon her son, and she said, O my lord, give her the living child, and in no wise slay it. But the other said, Let it be neither mine nor thine, but divide it.

Then the king answered and said, Give her the living child, and in no wise slay it: she is the mother thereof." When the story began, she was called a harlot, but by the conclusion, she was called the mother.

1 Kings 3:28 says, "And all Israel heard of the judgment which the king had judged; and they feared the king: for they saw that the wisdom of God was in him, to do judgment." It was Solomon's extreme measure that revealed the rightful mother. Here's how you can tell the difference between a lie and the truth: truth will never divide the baby. Truth is all or nothing. If you're selective about which scriptures you obey, believe, and agree with, then you're not seeking truth. Truth says, *"I want the whole baby. Don't split it up. Don't cut it in two. I want it all. I want the Gospels. I want the Epistles. I want Revelation. I want the Major Prophets. I want the Minor Prophets. I want the books of History and Poetry. I want the books of the Law. I want the Acts of the Apostles. I want it all."*

This is the dividing factor. The Word of God is the standard by which we prove all things. If you want to know what is true, bring out the sword—the Word of God. Hebrews 4:12 is a special scripture because it addresses all of humanity, the spirit world, and gives us a key to discerning and proving all things. "For the word of God is quick, and powerful, and sharper than any twoedged sword, piercing even to the dividing asunder of soul and spirit, and of the joints and marrow, and is a discerner of the thoughts and intents of the heart." —Hebrews 4:12

I want to focus specifically on the part that says, "piercing even to the dividing asunder of soul and spirit." The Word of God is sharper than any two-edged sword. This is why it's so important to know the scripture and have it hidden in your heart. Even if you don't fully understand it at the moment, you must have it memorized and buried deep within. When a false prophet or teacher tries to speak into your life, you can flip through the Rolodex of scripture in your heart and say, "But it is written." When the winds of false doctrine begin to blow, you can draw from the Word you've hidden away and declare, "But it is written... Thus saith the Lord..."*

You may not have all revelation and understanding, but when temptation arises, that verse you didn't fully grasp at first will rise up and protect you from lies. When the devil tries to convince you of something, the Word is quick to defend and shield you. When those around you try to sway your thinking, the Word you have carefully hidden in your heart will quicken you.

This is what Jesus meant when He said, "The Holy Ghost will come and bring all things to your remembrance whatsoever I have said unto you." I've had this happen on many occasions—whether while preaching, teaching the Word of God, dealing with a problem, or in casual conversation. Suddenly, scriptures would pour out of me—verses I hadn't planned to say, weren't in my notes, and sometimes didn't even remember memorizing. Sometimes I wonder if I had even read that particular verse before, but out it came. That's the Holy Spirit bringing all things to our remembrance. The Word of God is quick, powerful, and sharper than any two-edged sword. It's sharper than any book of literature you've ever read. It's sharper than anything you'll find at Barnes & Noble or on Google. It's sharper than any lecture given by a professor. It's sharper than anything from any expert in any field. The Word of God is sharper than any two-edged sword, piercing even to the dividing asunder of soul and spirit.

If we gathered a room full of people and asked each to describe the difference between the soul and the spirit, we'd get a colorful variety of answers. They're so similar, yet they're different. First of all, they're invisible, but they each have a unique role. The soul contains the conscience, the part of you where God can speak to you no matter how far you drift. Even when you've fallen, eaten the forbidden fruit, defied God, rejected Him, and run away like a heathen, at your lowest point, a word from God can reach you. God breathed into you the breath of life and gave you a conscience. You may have never heard the gospel preached, but you've got a soul with a conscience.

Then there's the spirit. The spirit is where emotions exist. Emotions and thoughts dwell within your spirit. The spirit can get off-kilter easily, and when it does, we say, "They've got a bad spirit," meaning, "They've got a bad attitude." It's the same thing. The spirit is the part of us that we own and operate. The soul is the part of us that God uses to communicate with us.

PROVE IT WITH THE WORD

Hebrews 4:12 tells us that the Word of God pierces to the dividing asunder of soul and spirit. The part of you that listens to God and the part of you that listens to yourself are so closely intertwined that only the Word of God can separate them. That's why people often say, "I didn't know if it was God speaking to me or if it was just me." The soul and spirit are so similar that we often can't tell the difference, but the Word of God divides them.

For example, when you read Psalm 119:113, "I hate vain thoughts: but thy law do I love," it reveals the division between your spirit's vain thoughts and your soul's desire to love God's law. Or Psalm 119:114, "Thou art my hiding place and my shield..."—your spirit might seek refuge in the bottle, your career, or even your family, but your soul knows that your true hope is in God's Word. Suddenly, the Word of God has divided the soul from the spirit, helping you to prove all things.

Psalm 119:115 says, "Depart from me, ye evildoers: for I will keep the commandments of my God." Some are wrestling with whether they should continue walking with certain people, and they need the Word of God to divide what their spirit wants from what their soul knows is right. The Word of God divides between soul and spirit, putting your spirit in its proper place—submitted to God's Word—so that your soul can rise up to worship the Lord and stay in constant communion with Him. This enables you to discern good from bad, to judge with understanding, and to prove all things by the help of God's holy Word.

This principle is a key to keeping evil from entering your life. Prove all things. If you run every decision through the scrutiny of spiritual discernment, you'll resist the appearance of evil. To abstain from all appearance of evil, put every "thing" through the rigorous trying of the Spirit. Let the washing of the Word cleanse your life of anything that shouldn't be there. When you're unsure whether a thought or feeling is of God, let the Word of God divide right from wrong, good from bad, and light from dark. This is the best way to keep evil out of your life, your home, and your relationship with God.

CHAPTER 8

CLING TO THE GOOD

HOLD FAST TO THE TRUTH

Sometimes, when we think of this scripture, we tend to interpret it as "hold fast to those things that are good." But what is that? Notice that it doesn't say, "those things that are good." It says, "that which is good." There is one thing that is good, and that is what we are to hold fast to. It's crucial to get it in our hearts that there is *that* which is good, and we must hold fast to it. What this world calls good is not good. In fact, the Bible describes this spiritual condition, and we are seeing it unfold before our eyes today.

Isaiah 5:20 says, "Woe unto them that call evil good, and good evil; that put darkness for light, and light for darkness; that put bitter for sweet, and sweet for bitter!"

This is what people are doing all around us, both inside and outside the church. This is why it is so important that we hold fast to that which is good, so that we can abstain from all appearance of evil. If we don't hold fast to that which is good, if we don't prove all things, if we're not praying without ceasing, if we're not rejoicing evermore, if we're not giving thanks in everything, if we're despising prophecies, if we're quenching the Spirit—then we will fall in line with this world, calling that which is evil good and that which is good evil. It is a total reversal of what is true and right. We must know the truth.

It's like those who work at the treasury. They don't need to know what a counterfeit looks like; they are so familiar with the real bill that they can easily spot a counterfeit. Their familiarity with the true item helps them catch the sham and phony. This is how we should be in our walk with God. We should be so tuned in to the truth that we can recognize the counterfeit when we see it, hear it, or feel it, and not be deceived by it. The Bible describes it as the "certain sound of truth." It is imperative that, as the word of God is preached, it has that certain sound of truth. Even if you can't put your finger on it, you can sense when something doesn't feel or sound right. Don't ignore that feeling. Investigate and understand whether what you're hearing is the truth.

I tell people all the time, "Don't just take my word—or any preacher's word—for what is being taught. Look into the Bible for yourself and really get it into your heart. You need to understand that this is the word of the Lord." I would also encourage other young preachers to be accurate when they preach, even in the smallest things. For example, I used to mistakenly refer to the Shunammite woman in the Old Testament as a widow, even though her husband is mentioned in the story. I often confused her with the widow of Zarephath. It's a minor mistake, but one I've been working on correcting. Accuracy is important. I've had moments where I said, "The Shunammite widow said to her husband," and saw people in the congregation smile or adjust themselves in their seats. I'm not talking about being overly critical, but as preachers, we're still human. Thank God for His mercy! I pray that I can always get it right and be accurate in my preaching.

Another instance occurred when I preached about the children of Israel wandering in the wilderness. It was only my second time preaching, and I made a statement about how they must have replaced their sandals, clothes, and tents during those 40 years. After the service, a seasoned preacher kindly pulled me aside and showed me from scripture that what I had said was inaccurate. I thought I had connected the dots, but I was mistaken. While it may seem like a minor detail, I don't want to build a ministry on inaccuracies. I'm thankful for someone who knew the word of the Lord and corrected me. This is why knowing the truth is so vital—not so we can be proud of our knowledge, but so we can recognize a lie when we hear it. Get into the Word, prove all things, and hold fast to that which is good.

If you don't, you will fall into the same deception that is sweeping the world. It's a frightening reality when so many are being deceived. We, as children of God, have a responsibility to remain blameless—not through our own righteousness, but through the righteousness of Jesus Christ. If we embrace evil, it corrupts that blamelessness. We are called to abstain from all appearance of evil, and we do that by holding fast to that which is good.

Mark 10:17-18 says, "And when he was gone forth into the way, there came one running, and kneeled to him, and asked him, Good Master, what shall I do that I may inherit eternal life? And Jesus said unto him, Why callest thou me good? There is none good but one, that is, God."

When I say we must hold fast to that which is good, I don't mean a random collection of "good" things. If we were to name things we consider "good," we might mention pumpkin pie, a walk on the beach, or a good book. But we need to understand that there is one good, and that is God Almighty. Nothing else compares to Him. What the world calls good is not good. What is good is God. Anything that is truly good reflects the Lord. It is not good in and of itself; it is good because God's Word sanctifies it, because His Spirit covers it, because it reflects Him, and because it is saturated with His power.

This is why in the book of Acts we find a situation where the apostles are having to make a rather weighty decision. As they're making these decisions, in their counseling with one another, the apostles are trying to determine what direction they should go. They said, "It seemeth good to the Holy Ghost." In other words they were running it through the scrutiny of the Spirit. They were causing it to go through the checks and the balances of the holy word of God. Does it measure up to God's priorities? Does it measure up to God's nature? Does it measure up to God's love? Does it measure up to God's integrity? Does it measure up to God's compassion? Does it measure up to God's commandment? If it does, then it is good to the Holy Spirit. If it's good to the Holy Spirit then it is good to us.

Let's go now to the first time we ever encounter in the word of God the use of the word good. Genesis 1:1-4, "In the beginning God created the heaven and the earth. 2. And the earth was without form, and void; and darkness was upon the face of the deep. And the Spirit of God moved upon the face of the waters. 3. And God said, Let there be light: and there was light. 4. And God saw the light, that it was good: and God divided the light from the darkness."

When God spoke that light into the Earth, God said, "Let there be light," and there was light, and when God saw the light, God said, "It is good." Now there is none good but God, so when he looked at that light after speaking that light and calling it good, he was saying, "Good. It's a proper reflection of me. I'm the only one that is good anywhere." God says that it is good because he looked at it. He saw what it did to the darkness. He saw that it dispelled the darkness. He saw how it eliminated darkness. He was able to divide it from the darkness. He called the light day and the darkness he called night and he said, "That's what I do. It is good. It is a proper reflection of me, and when people see light and they are seeing an example of me."

If you were to turn all the lights off through out the world. Everything everywhere would be dark. Until the sun would shine on us we wouldn't really see much at all. This is how it is in the physical, but in the spiritual world we would have to cover our face because his light is blinding. This is how God operates. The Lord is my light and my salvation. The Lord is your light and your salvation. Jesus said, "I am the light of the world," and then when he comes into us and we are baptized into him, he says, "You are the light of the world." This is how light becomes good because God has spoken it into the darkness of the earth and it is a reflection of what he does in the spirit.

Genesis 1:6-10, "And God said, Let there be a firmament in the midst of the waters, and let it divide the waters from the waters. 7. And God made the firmament, and divided the waters which were under the firmament from the waters which were above the firmament: and it was so. 8. And God called the firmament Heaven. And the evening and the morning were the second day. 9. And God said, Let the waters under the heaven be gathered together unto one place, and let the dry land appear: and it was so. 10. And God called the dry land Earth; and the gathering together of the waters called he Seas: and God saw that it was good."

It was and is a proper reflection of him because he is gathering together these waters. This is such an apt depiction of God. When you look at the mysteries that there are in God. As an experiment, I would pose the question to as many people as I could and see if they know every mystery about God. Of course, it's a trick question because we don't know everything that there is to know about God. There were times where waters were parted. The Red Sea was parted once. The Jordan river was parted three times. When we're baptized in Jesus name there is a displacement of the water as we are buried with him by baptism into his death. Here's the thing about waters. Waters cover and they make what is under them covered. The mystery remains, but when the waters are parted it is a type of revelation. It's an uncovering of what has always been there, but because we are not God we don't know about it. So when we are baptized in the name of Jesus Christ it is actually typifying what happens when we come into that great revelation of his name. We are being immersed into those things that we did not know until we came into this beautiful revelation of his name, his word, and his blood.

I can still remember the first time I understood that he loves me and he loved me even when I didn't know that he was loving me. I can remember when I first received the revelation of the oneness of the godhead. There are many great mysteries that are buried beneath the spiritual waters for so many people. At the same time, there are also a multitude of people that can point to the moment that God an to part those waters so that they could understand more of who he is, what he does, his nature, his voice, and his desires for us. Can you remember the moment when you first understood that he was coming back for a bride that had made herself ready and she was without spot, without wrinkle, and without blemish? You didn't know this before the waters were parted, but once the waters parted then you saw what was underneath.

Before the waters part you can be fearful. Nobody really likes navigating waters that they can't see what they are stepping in or stepping on. I've waded into some muddy waters. There's not a feeling in the world that will make your skin crawl like when you brush up against some UUO. That's an Unidentified Underwater Object. You want those waters to part so that you can understand what exactly is going on down there. God looked at the waters he gathered and said, "This is how I operate. It's a proper depiction of my Spirit." When the waters parted land appeared. Dry land appeared. Inhabitable land appeared. Understandable land appeared. All because the waters were parted. It was good because it was a reflection of him. He is the only thing that is good so this to was good. God did this throughout creation so that man can look at every part of creation and see reflections of God. There came a point where man couldn't properly hear the voice of God. So God encoded his message, which we call the gospel, the good news, the good message, and it is that which is good. That's the gospel. God encoded all creation with the good news. That's why when he created the light it was good. When he gathered the water it was good. It all reflected him.

Genesis 1:11-12 says, "And God said, Let the earth bring forth grass, the herb yielding seed, and the fruit tree yielding fruit after his kind, whose seed is in itself, upon the earth: and it was so. And the earth brought forth grass, and herb yielding seed after his kind, and the tree yielding fruit, whose seed was in itself, after his kind: and God saw that it was good."

When a seed goes down into the ground and breaks open, that's exactly what happened at Calvary and the days following. Jesus was broken on our behalf—not His bones, but His body was pierced for us. Just like a seed dies in the ground and bursts forth into life, Jesus was buried in the earth and rose again, bearing much fruit. We are that fruit. He is the first fruits, and we are the fruits of His resurrection power.

As God created the power of the seed to produce life after its kind, He said, "It is good because it is doing what I am going to do." He created life after His kind. In other words, we are like Jesus because of His death, burial, and resurrection power. That's why we preach, teach, sing, pray, and claim the power of the life, death, burial, and resurrection of Jesus Christ. We preach the blood, the Word, the name, and the Spirit because these are what have the power to set the human heart free. God looked at it and said, "It is good."

Genesis 1:14 says, "And God said, Let there be lights in the firmament of the heaven to divide the day from the night; and let them be for signs, and for seasons, and for days, and years."

These lights in the firmament divide the day from the night, and from this verse, we also see that time is God's creation. In the New Jerusalem, we will no longer be governed by time. Jesus will be the light, and there will be no night—no time. It will be a perpetual moment with no aging, no decay, and no longing for more time. We will simply be where He is, forevermore.

Genesis 1:15-18 continues, "And let them be for lights in the firmament of the heaven to give light upon the earth: and it was so. And God made two great lights; the greater light to rule the day, and the lesser light to rule the night: he made the stars also. And God set them in the firmament of the heaven to give light upon the earth, and to rule over the day and over the night, and to divide the light from the darkness: and God saw that it was good."

When God first created light, He said it was good. Now He speaks of the division of light and darkness, day and night. This is good because God is a stark contrast to the evil in this world. He is pure, holy, and righteous.

Genesis 1:20-21 says, "And God said, Let the waters bring forth abundantly the moving creature that hath life, and fowl that may fly above the earth in the open firmament of heaven. And God created great whales, and every living creature that moveth, which the waters brought forth abundantly, after their kind, and every winged fowl after his kind: and God saw that it was good."

This is one reason why God wanted to preserve these creatures on the ark. He created them to reflect His glory and power. Currently, they are part of a fallen earth, not fully reflecting Him as intended. They were never meant to be predators. We view it as the circle of life, but in the new earth, the wolf will lie down with the lamb. The lamb won't have to fear the wolf devouring it. Just as man will be redeemed from his predatory instincts, so will the animals. Everything God created was meant to reflect His glory, even the smallest creatures like ants, conies, and locusts. Paul said, "Doth not even nature itself teach you," because God put it there to teach us.

Psalm 19:1-2 says, "The heavens declare the glory of God; and the firmament sheweth his handywork. Day unto day uttereth speech, and night unto night sheweth knowledge."

I thank God for His word. Even if it were banned, and we could no longer read its pages, day after day, the earth speaks the word of God, and night after night reveals the wisdom and knowledge of Almighty God. You can see it. Step outside in the middle of the night and listen. Darkness has settled over everything. It is quiet and still. This reflects the burial of Jesus Christ—the Sabbath He spent in the grave. The night was made for rest. Thanks to Thomas Edison, we've extended our waking hours, but the night was designed for sleep. In just a few hours, the light will shine again upon the earth. This has happened every morning since Genesis 1. The sun never fails. You can count on it for a sunrise service, whether others join you or not. The sun will join you, rising in all its splendor, power, and glory. Every morning, the Lord proclaims, "Life, death, burial, and resurrection." Day after day, He shows us this truth: Life, death, burial, and resurrection.

Once the sun rises, it represents the resurrection—a reflection of both Jesus' resurrection and His birth. As the day progresses, it reflects His life. Be busy during the day; do what needs to be done. "Work while it is day, for the night comes when no man can work." When the sun goes down, let the day die and be buried, and let it be resurrected with new hope for another day. If things walked all over your nerves today and you're ready to give up, don't quit—just call it a night. Get some rest and try again tomorrow. There's new hope, new life, and new resurrection. God said, "It is good."

That's exactly how it works. He created the whales, and the water brought them forth. Interestingly, the waters also brought forth the winged creatures. This has deep symbolism connected to baptism because the winged creatures and the fish of the sea reflect how the Spirit operates—going into the deep waters and ascending into the heavens. When you're baptized in Jesus' name and come out of the water, you receive the gift of the Holy Ghost, enabling you to operate in the Spirit. God looked at it all and said, "That's good. I like it. It's good because I'm good, and it's a reflection of Me and how My Spirit and nature work."

Genesis 1:22-27 says, "And God blessed them, saying, Be fruitful, and multiply, and fill the waters in the seas, and let fowl multiply in the earth. And the evening and the morning were the fifth day. And God said, Let the earth bring forth the living creature after his kind, cattle, and creeping thing, and beast of the earth after his kind: and it was so. And God made the beast of the earth after his kind, and cattle after their kind, and every thing that creepeth upon the earth after his kind: and God saw that it was good. And God said, Let us make man in our image, after our likeness: and let them have dominion over the fish of the sea, and over the fowl of the air, and over the cattle, and over all the earth, and over every creeping thing that creepeth upon the earth. So God created man in his own image, in the image of God created he him; male and female created he them."

Some interpret this scripture to suggest God was speaking to someone else, but there is none good but one, and that is God. He wasn't speaking to another person. The Bible doesn't explain who He was addressing, so we don't need to speculate. Some suggest He was speaking to angels or using majestic pluralities, but the scripture makes it clear: one God said, "Let us make man in our image," and when He created man, He made one man. This one man reflects God's nature with three distinct components: body, soul, and spirit. Just as God is one Lord who manifests as Father, Son, and Holy Spirit, we are made in His image, having body, soul, and spirit. Our body reflects Jesus, who walked the earth in flesh and blood. We have a soul because God breathed life into us, making us living souls, not just living bodies. The missing piece to becoming one with God is being regenerated by the Holy Spirit.

When we repent, we reconcile with God in soul. When we are baptized in Jesus' name, we reconcile with Him in body. When we are filled with His Spirit, we reconcile with Him in spirit. He is not three persons; He is one God, and Jesus Christ is the express image of His person. God said, "Let us make man in our image," and He created one man in the image of one God—complete with body, soul, and spirit. Male and female are created in the image of God.

Genesis 1:28 says, "And God blessed them, and God said unto them, Be fruitful, and multiply, and replenish the earth, and subdue it: and have dominion over the fish of the sea, and over the fowl of the air, and over every living thing that moveth upon the earth."

This is why male-male and female-female marriages are not of God. Male and female together reflect the nature of God. That union has the divine power to generate an eternal soul, one of the most awesome powers on earth. It reflects God's life-creating nature. When a man and woman are married, they become one because God is one. This is a beautiful illustration of Jesus Christ and His bride, the church.

Genesis 1:29-31 continues, "And God said, Behold, I have given you every herb bearing seed, which is upon the face of all the earth, and every tree, in the which is the fruit of a tree yielding seed; to you it shall be for meat. And to every beast of the earth, and to every fowl of the air, and to every thing that creepeth upon the earth, wherein there is life, I have given every green herb for meat: and it was so. And God saw every thing that he had made, and, behold, it was very good. And the evening and the morning were the sixth day."

The word "very" means "truly" or "truth." It's where we get the word "verify" and even the word "verb," which signifies action. Actions reveal the truth. You can say what you want, but if your actions don't align with your words, it's not true. When God said, "It is very good," He was saying, "This is truth. It reflects My nature."

When the apostle Paul, under the inspiration of the Holy Spirit, says, "Hold fast that which is good," he is speaking of the truth that has been the bedrock of the earth. Hold fast to the truth of God, to His mighty power, to what He has done in the earth. Hold fast to the truth of His divine nature. Hold fast to that which is good. One of the areas that refers to "that which is good" is when Paul speaks of the gospel. We tend to read the word gospel without fully grasping its weight, but it's essential to hold fast to it because it is the truth.

Romans 1:16 says, "For I am not ashamed of the gospel of Christ: for it is the power of God unto salvation to everyone that believeth; to the Jew first, and also to the Greek."

What Paul was saying is, "I am not ashamed of that good message of Jesus Christ." It's not just a message that has good things mixed into it. God doesn't mix—God separates. His message is the only good message. It's not about saying, "That was a good sermon," or "She had a good day," or "He had a good time." There's only one who is truly good, and that is God. The message of Jesus Christ is good. The message that He lived the life we were supposed to live but couldn't, is good. The message that He died the death we deserved to die, in our place, is good. The message that He was buried in a borrowed tomb and rose from the dead, victorious over death, hell, and the grave, is very good. That message is the goodness—the good news—the gospel of Jesus Christ. So, hold fast to that.

As you walk through this life, you will encounter evil along the way. There will be evil in the grocery store, evil in the people you meet, evil in many places you look. Paul admonished us, "Abstain from all appearance of evil." The way to do that is by holding fast to that which is good. Hold fast to it. Jesus bought me and sought me with His redeeming blood. He loved me before I even knew Him, and all my love is due to Him. He plunged me to victory beneath the cleansing flood. This is what holding fast to that which is good looks like: Victory in Jesus, my Savior, forever. Jesus paid it all, and all to Him I owe. Sin had left a crimson stain, but He washed it white as snow.

I'm holding fast to that which is good. On a hill far away stood an old rugged cross, the emblem of suffering and shame. I love that old cross, where the dearest and best for a world of lost sinners was slain. I will cling to the old rugged cross and exchange it one day for a crown. When gloom and sadness whisper, "You've sinned, there's no use to pray," turn and look to Jesus—that's holding fast to that which is good. He tells me, "I see a crimson stream of blood that flows from Calvary. Its waves reach the throne of God and they're sweeping over me." These songs were written by people who knew how to hold fast to that which is good. They were born out of revelation as the waters parted, revealing the truth beneath.

I'm holding fast to that which is good. When someone says, "Don't you know what the doctors said?" the response should be, "Yes, I know what the doctors said, but the prophet Isaiah said, 'By His stripes, we are healed,' and I'm holding fast to that which is good." When doubt and fear creep in saying, "Don't you know you're going through the worst season of your life?" the answer should be, "I may be going through the worst season, but I will not be weary in well-doing, for in due season, I will reap if I faint not. I'm holding fast to that which is good, and the Lord knows how to deliver the godly out of temptation."

The phrase "holding fast" means to hold it down, memorize it, and get it in your heart. We need to learn the truth so well that nothing can take it away from us. Do you know how many times the Bible has been banned, burned, or removed from bookshelves? They can take it from shelves, libraries, schools, and even churches, but they cannot take it from our hearts. Memorize this book. Hold fast to that which is good.

Psalm 27:4 says, "One thing have I desired of the Lord, that will I seek after; that I may dwell in the house of the LORD all the days of my life, to behold the beauty of the LORD, and to inquire in His temple."

Luke 10:38-42 tells the story of Martha and Mary: "Now it came to pass, as they went, that Jesus entered into a certain village, and a certain woman named Martha received Him into her house. And she had a sister called Mary, who also sat at Jesus' feet and heard His word. But Martha was distracted with much serving, and came to Him and said, 'Lord, do you not care that my sister has left me to serve alone? Tell her to help me.' But Jesus answered and said to her, 'Martha, Martha, you are worried and troubled about many things. But one thing is needed, and Mary has chosen that good part, which will not be taken away from her.'"

Martha, busy around the house, said to Jesus, "Lord, tell Mary to help me in the kitchen." Jesus responded, "Martha, thank you. I'm sure the meal will be delicious, and you are careful and troubled about many things, but Mary has chosen the good part, and it will not be taken away." To the Marthas of today: when distractions, health, wealth, or friends are taken away, there is still a good part that shall not be taken away.

THE GOODNESS AND GREATNESS OF GOD

We often talk about how great God is—and He is great. He is great and greatly to be praised. I love the childhood prayer many of us were taught: "God is great. God is good. Let us thank Him for our food. By His hands, we are fed. Thank you, Lord, for our daily bread. Amen." Sometimes, though, I think we forget that God isn't just great—He is good. We know He's great. We know He's going to take His children to heaven. We know He prepared a place for us and will bring us there one day. But sometimes we forget that He's not just great—He's also good.

He looks after the little things. He sees every sparrow that falls. He's so good that He numbers the very hairs on our heads. That's how closely He pays attention to what we're going through. He is good. So hold fast to that which is good. Let go of the temporal things, the carnal things, and the wicked things. Hold fast to the one who is good. Hold fast to the good news of His gospel. Hold fast to that which is good.

Romans 11:22 says, "Behold therefore the goodness and severity of God: on them which fell, severity; but toward thee, goodness, if thou continue in his goodness: otherwise thou also shalt be cut off."

The Bible describes something powerful: the goodness and the severity of God. These two things are connected. Often, we shy away from His severity because it scares us. But take note of that word, "severity," because it comes from the word "sever." Sometimes the most good God will ever do for you is to sever whatever evil is trying to destroy you. It hurts—it's painful—because the evil becomes attached to you, becomes a part of you. If you have a tumor wrapped around an organ, it must be removed, even though the process will be painful. The doctors will anesthetize you, cut you open, and go to places inside of you that you've never seen but that are killing you.

THE POWER OF GOD'S WORD

Hebrews 4:12 says, "For the word of God is quick, and powerful, and sharper than any two-edged sword, piercing even to the dividing asunder of soul and spirit, and of the joints and marrow, and is a discerner of the thoughts and intents of the heart."

When you place yourself in the hands of the Great Physician, our Savior who can save to the uttermost, He uses His word like a surgical instrument, sharper than any two-edged sword. He cuts what needs to be cut and leaves what needs to remain. He severs what needs to be severed and restores what needs to be restored. When you come out of it, recovery will hurt at first. It won't be easy to get up and walk around. You'll have to relearn some things, take time to rest, and regain your strength and mobility. As uncomfortable as the process may be, it's the goodness of God at work in your life.

I wish I had the power to help every man, woman, and child embrace the goodness of God right now. The next time you go to the Lord in prayer, say, "God, I may not understand it, but I know that You are good. One thing I am determined to do is hold fast to the one constant good in the universe, and I know that it is You."

CHAPTER 9

ABSTAIN FROM ALL APPEARANCE OF EVIL

We've been examining the passage of scripture found in 1 Thessalonians 5, which I've referred to as "bullet points." These brief and direct admonitions from the apostle Paul are powerful lessons for the church. Let's revisit them. 1 Thessalonians 5:16-24, "Rejoice evermore. 17. Pray without ceasing. 18. In everything give thanks: for this is the will of God in Christ Jesus concerning you. 19. Quench not the Spirit. 20. Despise not prophesyings. 21. Prove all things; hold fast that which is good."

THE COMMAND TO ABSTAIN FROM EVIL

Now, we arrive at verse 22, which is the culminating admonition: **"Abstain from all appearance of evil." This is not just an idle suggestion from the apostle Paul—it's a command for Christian living. It's important because evil is what undermines our walk with God. It's what keeps us from being blameless in His sight. If you examine the story of humanity from the very beginning, you will find that evil is what robbed us of our blameless state before the Lord. Adam and Eve were blameless until they disobeyed God and ate from the tree of the knowledge of good and evil. That one act of rebellion introduced sin into the world, making humanity culpable. We've been dealing with the consequences of that ever since. For us, the goal is clear: to abstain from all appearance of evil. But the question we need to answer is how.

How can we avoid the very appearance of evil in a world filled with temptation and sin? How can we, as Christians, live blamelessly before the Lord? The purpose of this book is to explore these questions and point us toward a life that reflects Christ. The "bullet points" Paul gives us in 1 Thessalonians 5 are practical steps toward achieving this goal. These admonitions help us build a life that avoids evil and its traps. But there's a challenge—many people today don't know how to recognize evil. In fact, our society often struggles to define what is evil and what is good. We live in a time, as Isaiah prophesied, where people call evil good and good evil (Isaiah 5:20). The lines between right and wrong have become blurred, and the ability to discern the difference has diminished. If we try to define evil based solely on our own understanding or cultural standards, we will inevitably fall short. And worse, we may find ourselves engaging in evil without even realizing it.

EVIL IN ACTION

So how do we recognize evil? The Bible offers us clear examples, and while we cannot cover every instance of evil mentioned in scripture, we can look at some key examples that illuminate this concept.

One of the clearest examples comes from the life of Joseph,

particularly in the actions of his brothers. Genesis 50:19-20 tells us, "Fear not: for am I in the place of God? But as for you, ye thought evil against me; but God meant it unto good..." Joseph's brothers betrayed him, sold him into slavery, and plotted evil against him out of jealousy. The Bible uses the word "evil" repeatedly to describe their actions. But what led them down this path of evil? Let's trace it back.

Genesis 37:2-4 gives us insight into the roots of their actions, "Joseph, being seventeen years old, was feeding the flock with his brethren... and Joseph brought unto his father their evil report. Now Israel loved Joseph more than all his children... and he made him a coat of many colors. And when his brethren saw that their father loved him more than all his brethren, they hated him, and could not speak peaceably unto him."

Joseph's brothers despised him not only because of their father's favoritism but because Joseph had dreams that seemed self-serving. Their hatred began to fester. Here's where we see the danger: hate and jealousy unchecked will always lead to evil. What started as resentment in their hearts turned into a full-blown conspiracy.

Genesis 37:17-19 shows this progression, "And Joseph went after his brethren, and found them in Dothan. And when they saw him afar off, even before he came near unto them, they conspired against him to slay him. And they said one to another, Behold, this dreamer cometh."

Their initial thoughts were evil, and they quickly acted upon them. When Joseph approached, they seized the opportunity to harm him, ultimately selling him into slavery. This is an important lesson: if Joseph's brothers had abstained from the very appearance of evil, their story would have been vastly different. If they had recognized the evil thoughts forming in their hearts, they could have resisted them.

But instead, their unchecked hatred led them to commit a grievous sin against their brother.

Joseph's story also provides a contrasting example of righteousness. When faced with temptation from Potiphar's wife, Joseph fled. He chose to abstain from the appearance of evil. Because of his faithfulness, he was later in a position to forgive his brothers. His life shows us that when we abstain from evil, we not only protect ourselves but also keep ourselves in a position to show grace to others.

This brings us to a critical point: evil begins in the heart. Jesus taught that it's not just our actions that matter but our thoughts and intentions as well. Matthew 15:19 says, "For out of the heart proceed evil thoughts, murders, adulteries, fornications, thefts, false witness, blasphemies." If we do not deal with evil at its root—in the heart—it will eventually manifest in our actions. That's why Paul instructs us to abstain from even the appearance of evil. We must deal with sin at its earliest stages before it takes root.

Another powerful example is Saul's pursuit of David. Saul's jealousy and rebellion against God opened the door to evil in his heart. As a result, evil spirits tormented him. At one point, Saul had made it illegal for witches to practice witchcraft in Israel, yet later in his life, he sought out a witch for guidance. This is what evil does—it takes you further than you ever intended to go and keeps you longer than you ever intended to stay. Saul's fall from grace was tragic, and it all began when he allowed evil into his heart.

The Bible is clear: evil is deceptive. It doesn't announce itself boldly—it sneaks in through unchecked emotions, through small compromises, and through rationalizations. That's why Paul's command to abstain from all appearance of evil is so crucial. We must guard our hearts and be vigilant in recognizing evil, even when it appears harmless. Sin often disguises itself as something small or insignificant, but it always leads to greater destruction.

As believers, we have been called to live blameless lives before God, not through our own righteousness but through the righteousness of Jesus Christ. 1 Peter 1:16 reminds us of this call, "Be ye holy; for I am holy." Holiness involves more than avoiding sin—it means actively pursuing God's standard of righteousness in every area of our lives. By embracing prayer, rejoicing, gratitude, discernment, and the other principles we've discussed throughout this book, we position ourselves to abstain from evil and to live lives that reflect Christ's light in a dark world.

So let us take Paul's words to heart and *abstain from all appearance of evil*. By recognizing evil for what it is and turning away from it, we can walk blamelessly before the Lord, free from the corruption of sin and full of the life-giving power of the Spirit.

Numbers 13:30-33, "And Caleb stilled the people before Moses, and said, Let us go up at once, and possess it; for we are well able to overcome it. But the men that went up with him said, We be not able to go up against the people; for they are stronger than we. And they brought up an evil report of the land which they had searched unto the children of Israel, saying, The land, through which we have gone to search it, is a land that eateth up the inhabitants thereof; and all the people that we saw in it are men of a great stature. And there we saw the giants, the sons of Anak, which come of the giants: and we were in our own sight as grasshoppers, and so we were in their sight."

The Israelites didn't even realize they were giving an evil report. They thought they were only stating their opinions, honestly assessing the situation, but they were really bringing up an evil report. What they were saying was in direct conflict with the promises of God.

Perhaps they knew this and ignored it, or maybe they truly didn't realize the danger of what they were doing. Either way, God did not send them into the land of promise to decide if His word would come to pass. He sent them to assess how the children of Israel could take possession of the land. It was a matter of forming strategy, not questioning the possibility of God's promises. Anything that contradicts God's word is an evil report.

God wasn't asking, "Am I God enough, strong enough, or good enough to do what I said I would do?" That wasn't the issue. He wanted them to plan for taking hold of the promise, not debate whether it could be done. But they came back saying, "We can't do it." They saw giants, they saw obstacles, and they lost confidence—not just in themselves, but in God. They said, "We're like grasshoppers in our own sight, and in theirs too." It's one thing to lose confidence in yourself, but don't ever lose confidence in God. He can and will do what He says. Their words became an evil report, and this is why we must *abstain from all appearance of evil*.

When David sinned with Bathsheba and orchestrated the death of her husband, Uriah, he allowed evil into his life. 2 Samuel 11:15-17, "And he wrote in the letter, saying, Set ye Uriah in the forefront of the hottest battle, and retire ye from him, that he may be smitten, and die. And it came to pass, when Joab observed the city, that he assigned Uriah unto a place where he knew that valiant men were. And the men of the city went out, and fought with Joab: and there fell some of the people of the servants of David; and Uriah the Hittite died also."

David, consumed by his own lust and blinded by sin, devised a cold, calculated plan to eliminate Uriah. This was not the same David we read about before. He had once been a man after God's own heart, but he did not abstain from the appearance of evil. David should have been on the battlefield with his men, but instead, he stayed behind. He should have turned his gaze away from Bathsheba, but he didn't. Evil doesn't always come with a roar—it can come quietly, like Bathsheba on her rooftop. David allowed what seemed like harmless temptation to spiral into one of the darkest moments of his life.

When David could not recognize the depth of his sin, God sent the prophet Nathan to confront him. Nathan told him a parable in 2 Samuel 12:1-4, "And the LORD sent Nathan unto David. And he came unto him, and said unto him, There were two men in one city; the one rich, and the other poor. The rich man had exceeding many flocks and herds: but the poor man had nothing, save one little ewe lamb, which he had bought and nourished up: and it grew up together with him, and with his children; it did eat of his own meat, and drank of his own cup, and lay in his bosom, and was unto him as a daughter. And there came a traveler unto the rich man, and he spared to take of his own flock and of his own herd, to dress for the wayfaring man that was come unto him; but took the poor man's lamb, and dressed it for the man that was come to him."

David's response was one of outrage, 2 Samuel 12:5-6, "And David's anger was greatly kindled against the man; and he said to Nathan, As the LORD liveth, the man that hath done this thing shall surely die: And he shall restore the lamb fourfold, because he did this thing, and because he had no pity."

David was ready to pass judgment without realizing that the parable was about him. Nathan then pointed at David and said, "You are the man." Only when he saw his sin from another perspective did David grasp the gravity of what he had done. **2 Samuel 12:9** reveals the core issue: Nathan asked, "Why have you despised the commandment of the Lord, to do evil in His sight?"

THE ROLE OF SPIRITUAL DISCERNMENT

David's story reminds us that evil doesn't always announce itself boldly. It can sneak in subtly, disguised as temptation or small compromises. But God's command remains: *Abstain from all appearance of evil*. David's failure to do this led him down a destructive path, but by God's grace and through repentance, he found forgiveness.

Let us learn from these examples. Whether it's the evil report of the Israelites or David's moral failure, we must be vigilant in guarding our hearts and minds. Evil can present itself in many forms, but with the guidance of God's word and the Spirit, we can recognize it and abstain from it, living blamelessly before the Lord.

This is why it is so challenging for people to abstain from all appearance of evil—because evil often appears, and they have no idea what it really is. They stumble, bumble, and mumble into evil without realizing that it surrounds them. Evil intoxicates them, swallows them up, and pulls them into its snare. They don't recognize it because they've satisfied the lust of their own flesh. They don't see it until they're on the outside, looking in on someone else's circumstances. Then they see the injustice, then they see the sin. It's often why people engaged in certain sins become harsh judges of others in the same sin. Some of the meanest critics are those deeply involved in the same actions. We must be careful, lest we find ourselves in the same position, unaware of the danger. We need open and honest hearts before God so that He can change our ways.

THE POWER OF THE WORD

This is why the preaching of the Word is so important. This is why Nathan's prophecy was so crucial for David. The Word of God helps us see things from the right perspective. It pricks our hearts and changes our lives. We see this on the Day of Pentecost. While Peter preached, he told the crowd, "You have taken this same Jesus and crucified Him." Many in the crowd likely thought the Romans alone were responsible for the crucifixion—the Romans nailed Him to the cross, mocked Him, pierced His side, and laid a crown of thorns on His head. But Peter said, "With wicked hands, you have crucified and slain Him." When they heard this, the Bible says they were "pricked in their hearts." This is what the preaching of the Word of God does—it reveals evil for what it is.

I learned long ago to just preach the Word. Do what the Spirit says. Preach the Word, and obey the Spirit. Someone always needs to hear what God is trying to say. You don't need to single people out in the congregation; the Lord can do it better than anyone. I preach what the Lord gives me, and the Spirit of the Lord does the rest—rightly. The preaching of the Word of God allows us to see evil for what it is. It helps us become more spiritually in tune than we've ever been. We grow closer to God, more knowledgeable of His Word. We begin to see evil clearly. We recognize it, confront it, and label it as evil. What do we do when we hear it? We don't turn up the volume. What do we do when we see it? We don't allow it to infiltrate the windows of our soul. We *abstain*. We determine, "No, I will not go there. I will not do that. I will not be involved. That is evil, trying to destroy my faith."

Some try to turn this admonition of abstaining from all appearance of evil into legalism. They say, "If you focus too much on this verse, you're being heavy-handed." They argue, "Haven't you heard of Christian liberty?" Are you kidding me? Abstaining from evil is one of the most merciful messages in the Bible! God doesn't want

His people stumbling blindly into evil, unaware of what it looks like or sounds like. That is not the kind of God I serve, and I wouldn't serve Him if that were His protocol. Instead, He puts His Word in the mouths of prophets and apostles, and they cry out, "Abstain from all appearance of evil."

Let me be clear—it's nearly impossible to list every form, shape, or appearance of evil in 2024. You can't draft a catalog that holds every possibility of evil in today's world. There are too many apps, too many downloads, too many social media profiles, conversations, thoughts, and emotions flying in every direction. You and I need *spiritual discernment*. We need conviction. We need hearts that are right with God. We need to be so sensitive to the voice of God that when He speaks, we obey. I want God to speak to me: "Abstain. Move away. Flee. Separate yourself from the workers of iniquity."

THE FOUNDATION: LAYER UPON LAYER

We've been talking about the foundational layers in 1 Thessalonians 5. We've explored them in depth, but let's go through them one last time to see how they help us abstain from all appearance of evil.

Rejoicing evermore helps you abstain from all appearance of evil and preserves you blameless because it brings a calm wellness to your soul. A great example is the Shunammite woman. Her promised son lay dead, but when asked how she was, she said, "It is well." Her circumstances were anything but well, but her faith spoke otherwise. Rejoicing evermore means choosing to say, "It is well," despite the circumstances. It doesn't mean that problems don't need solving or obstacles don't need overcoming—it means your response to every situation is rooted in faith that God is in control. When you declare

"It is well," you are choosing to stay anchored in God, refusing to let bitterness or disappointment define you.

The apostle Paul is so adamant about rejoicing because he lived it. He endured shipwrecks, beatings, rejection, and persecution, yet he said, "Rejoice in the Lord always, and again I say rejoice." Not sometimes. Not when things are going well. Always. Even when evil comes in the form of bitterness, unforgiveness, or envy, rejoicing allows you to declare, "No, it is well with my soul."

Praying without ceasing also helps you abstain from all appearance of evil. Prayer connects you to God, giving you strength to recognize and resist the enemy's schemes. There's an old hymn that says, "O what peace we often forfeit, O what needless pain we bear, all because we do not carry everything to God in prayer." When we pray, we place ourselves in God's hands, trusting Him to guide us away from evil and keep us close to Him. As we continue through 1 Thessalonians 5, each point builds upon the last, leading us to a life that abstains from all appearance of evil.

Carrying grudges, holding onto hurt feelings, or nurturing an offended spirit are clear manifestations of embracing the appearance of evil. You simply cannot carry those things and simultaneously carry the cross of Christ. Jesus invites us to crucify those sinful tendencies in prayer. When we verbalize our intention to let go of ungodly feelings and desires, we are actively crucifying them at the altar.

When we come before the Lord, it's important to lay these burdens down. If you're struggling to release them, don't give up. Keep praying, keep verbalizing their death, and ask the Lord to help you walk away from them. This is what it means to pray without ceasing—to continually seek God's help until we find victory. The Bible tells us, "Submit yourselves therefore to God. Resist the devil, and he will flee from you." Submission is key. You cannot resist the devil without first submitting to God, and prayer is the fastest way to do that.

Give thanks in everything—this isn't just advice, it's a command. Thanksgiving is a powerful defense against evil. When you're thankful for what you have, you're less likely to be enticed by what you don't have. Gratitude closes the door on temptation. It keeps our hearts humble and focused on God's provision, rather than the deceitful allure of sin.

Think of stealing. When we think of theft, we imagine someone in a mask holding up a store. But theft can also be more subtle—cutting corners, cheating others, lying to get ahead. Yet when we cultivate a heart of thanksgiving, we recognize that God provides for all our needs. Why would we need to steal when our Heavenly Father promises to supply everything we need? If God hasn't provided something for us, it means we don't need it, and if He hasn't provided a righteous way to attain it, we certainly don't need it. Gratitude keeps us grounded in this truth.

Could you imagine holding a garage sale for everything in your life that God didn't provide? It would probably be eye-opening. When we give thanks for our spouse, our job, our church family, and the blessings God has placed in our lives, we can abstain from the pull of evil thoughts—thoughts like jealousy, bitterness, and entitlement. These are the seeds of evil that, if allowed to take root, can grow into something much worse. We must choose to let go of these things and be justified by the blood of Jesus rather than by our own sense of self-righteousness.

When you reflect on what God has done, you realize there's nothing to complain about. Yes, life is challenging, but God is always good. Even in a world that is cursed and fallen, God's creation continues to yield fruit. The earth is dying, yet God, in His mercy, continues to sustain it and provide for us. This simple truth alone should inspire constant gratitude.

I've been blessed to hear from people who prayed for me without my knowing it—prayers that intervened in moments of difficulty, when I wasn't even aware I needed help. This is a perfect example of God's grace. I didn't deserve it, and yet God continues to be good. This is why I have no reason to complain. I'm thankful for His Word, His blessings, and His mercy. If we really stop and think about it, we can all find countless reasons to give thanks in everything.

Count your blessings—the elders would say. Name them one by one. Be intentional in your gratitude. Start small, if you have to, but you'll find that the list of things to thank God for never runs out. And when we live in this constant state of gratitude, we become much more adept at spotting evil and resisting its allure. You won't entertain bitterness, envy, or anger when your heart is focused on the goodness of God. Instead, you'll realize that you're not missing out on anything by walking in obedience to Him.

The Bible says, "Enter ye in at the strait gate: for wide is the gate, and broad is the way, that leadeth to destruction... But strait is the gate, and narrow is the way, which leadeth unto life" (Matthew 7:13-14). The narrow way may not be popular, and it may seem that others are having more fun, but remember: they are not on a path you want to follow. Walking with God is the greatest privilege we have, and it's a privilege we should be thankful for every day.

And that narrow path includes walking in love with your brothers and sisters in Christ. You may not always like everyone who is walking with you, but you must love them. Scripture makes it clear: if you say you love God but hate your brother, you are a liar. You cannot love God, whom you have not seen, if you hate those around you, whom you see every day. If you struggle with this, go to God in prayer. He will help you, through continual prayer, rejoicing, and giving thanks, to overcome these feelings and truly love as He loves.

Rejoice evermore—this command is tied to everything we've been discussing. It means finding joy in every circumstance, not because everything is perfect, but because we trust in God's perfect plan. Paul, who endured more hardship than most of us can imagine, still said, "Rejoice in the Lord always: and again I say, Rejoice" (Philippians 4:4). This wasn't just advice; it was the key to Paul's ability to persevere through shipwrecks, beatings, and imprisonment.

When evil comes in the form of resentment, unforgiveness, or envy, rejoicing in the Lord gives us the strength to resist it. We can say, "It is well with my soul," not because our circumstances are ideal, but because we trust in the God who is with us in every trial. Rejoicing reminds us that our story is not over and that God's promises are still in effect. It keeps us from embracing anything that is contrary to His will.

Finally, we must pray without ceasing. This continual connection with God keeps us in tune with His voice, strengthens us to resist evil, and helps us navigate life's challenges with grace. Prayer aligns our hearts with God's and keeps us from falling into sin. It is our lifeline, our source of strength, and our weapon against the enemy.

Abstaining from all appearance of evil isn't just about avoiding sin; it's about cultivating a heart and life that seeks after God in everything. Through rejoicing, praying, and giving thanks, we walk the narrow path, free from the snares of evil, and closer to the One who calls us to Himself.

"Quench not the Spirit." I'm telling you; this is one of the most important parts of this passage. When the Spirit moves on you, don't quench it. The Spirit moves in unique ways, and when it prompts you with a, "No, that's wrong. Don't do it," don't ignore that. When the Spirit says, "You don't need to be here. You need to leave," don't quench that voice. The Spirit convicts your heart in real-time, often when you're not even recognizing evil for what it is. The Holy Spirit sharpens your understanding so that you become aware when you're engaging in, or entertaining, the appearance of evil. It's a slippery slope, and once you start down that path, it's hard to stop. Do not quench the Spirit.

One of the reasons I'm so thankful to be Apostolic Pentecostal is that we encourage the free flow of the Holy Spirit. You know why? Because powerful things happen in those moments. Lives change when the Spirit is allowed to move freely. Don't underestimate the power of an experience with God. Can you recall times when you were overwhelmed in His presence—times when you couldn't stop crying, speaking in tongues, or worshiping? You may not even remember what triggered it, but you know the Holy Spirit was moving. Don't quench it. You are missing out on some of the greatest blessings of your life if you stifle the Spirit when it moves upon you.

Sometimes, the Spirit will have you laugh when you expect to cry, or cry when you expect to laugh. It overtakes you in a way that transcends human emotions, and you're left thinking, "I'm just so happy," while tears are pouring down your face. Don't stifle that move of the Spirit. Those kinds of encounters with God can burn out cravings and sins that have plagued you for years. An attitude that's been destroying your peace can be vanquished in an instant if you allow the Spirit of the living God to have His way.

By not quenching the Spirit, you prepare yourself to abstain from all appearance of evil. Your spiritual senses become sharper. Just as you might have quick reflexes to danger in the natural—like leaping away from a snake without thinking—your spiritual reflexes can become automatic, too. You just know when something is wrong, without needing to deliberate. You know when you shouldn't watch something or go somewhere, and you quickly decide, "No, I'm not going there. I won't engage in that conversation." You develop a spiritual instinct to reject what is evil and embrace what is right.

I believe one of the greatest helps God has given us to avoid evil is through pastors and preachers. I don't say this because I am one, but because of the importance of hearing the word of God preached. Preaching and teaching are serious matters. The word of life is so powerful—it can deliver anyone from anything. I've seen it work in ways that leave no doubt in my mind. I've witnessed hearts soften as the word was preached, and I've seen lives change. This is why Paul says, "Despise not prophesyings." When the word goes forth, receive it. It's not random—it's prayed over and interceded for. God is reaching for someone's soul every time. And if, while listening, you think, "I sure hope they heard that," that's your cue—it was meant for you.

Every word that's preached is for you. Every word that's preached is for me. This word is so alive, so powerful. The Bible says it is spirit and it is life. That's why you can read the same scripture you've heard preached a hundred times, and yet still receive new revelation from it. Because it's alive and quickens our hearts.

Don't despise the word when it crosses you up. The word isn't something you can dismiss when it makes you uncomfortable. It's like the sign at the gym that says, "At first sign of discomfort, discontinue use." That's how some treat the word of God, but we can't approach scripture that way. The word challenges us to grow, and growth often comes with discomfort. Paul said in 2 Timothy 4:2-4,

"Preach the word; be instant in season, out of season; reprove, rebuke, exhort with all longsuffering and doctrine... For the time will come when they will not endure sound doctrine; but after their own lusts shall they heap to themselves teachers, having itching ears." Woe unto us if we only look to scripture for comfort and ignore its correction!

When David sinned with Bathsheba and orchestrated the death of Uriah, the consequences were severe. But I'm thankful David didn't despise the prophetic word when Nathan confronted him. Nathan could have been met with resistance, but instead, David humbled himself before God. He embraced the correction, repented, and it marked a turning point in his life. Though he had done something horrible, David did not continue down the path of evil. He allowed the word of God to humble him, and he abstained from further wickedness.

This is the power of not despising the word of God. Even when it conflicts with our desires or exposes our wrongs, we must embrace it. It is our lifeline to staying on the path of righteousness and avoiding the pitfalls of evil. When we hear the word, we should respond like David, with humility and repentance, allowing it to guide us back to God.

Let's not forget that the preaching of the word, the prophesyings, and the move of the Spirit are God's means of leading us away from evil and toward righteousness. Quench not the Spirit. Despise not prophesyings. Let the word do its work in your life, even when it's uncomfortable, because that's what will ultimately help you abstain from all appearance of evil.

Verse 21 tells us to prove all things. Don't just accept everything at face value. Let's get rid of the statement, "But everybody's doing it." Can we erase that from our vocabulary as a justification for anything? Everybody's doing it. Who cares? You are called to prove all things. You are called to discern what is the will of God—what is holy or unholy, right or wrong—and do it with honesty. Don't cater to the lust of your flesh, the lust of your eyes, or the pride of life. Do what pleases the Lord. Prove all things; hold fast that which is good. Cling to the old rugged cross. Hold fast to the good news and glorious gospel of Jesus Christ, which can save the sinner from their sin. Hold fast to the message that delivers the bound from bondage. Cling to the Gospel that raises the guilty from their fall. Hold fast to the blood of Jesus Christ. Hold fast to the love of Almighty God. Hold fast to the message that Jesus saves.

This isn't just fancy words or good ideas; it's real power. Real power. Not just mental power or positive attitude, but heavenly, Holy Spirit power. We've got to hold onto that which is good. This helps us abstain from all appearance of evil. Evil is so tricky and subtle. Think about the serpent in the Garden of Eden—it was never directly identified as the Devil in Genesis. Nor does it explicitly say the serpent is the Devil throughout the rest of Genesis or the Old Testament. We understand who it was—it's clear to us now. But the Bible doesn't specifically tell us the serpent is the Devil until Revelation 12:9: "And the great dragon was cast out, that old serpent, called the Devil, and Satan, which deceiveth the whole world: he was cast out into the earth, and his angels were cast out with him."

If you approach this as a complete stranger to the Word of God, without prior knowledge, you wouldn't encounter the serpent until three chapters into the Bible, and you wouldn't know it was the Devil until near the end of Revelation. That's amazing to me! The reason God didn't make a big issue of the Devil being a serpent is because He knew that's how Satan would always operate—subtly. The Devil is a snake, but sometimes he comes as a lion, a bear, or in the form of temptation, like Delilah or Sheba. Sometimes it's a spirit you can't see, smell, or hear, but he's there. You need to know evil when it shows up, so you can abstain from it and help your family abstain from it. By practicing these principles—rejoicing evermore, praying without ceasing, in everything giving thanks, quenching not the Spirit, despising not prophesying, and proving all things—you will be able to abstain from all appearance of evil.

1 Thessalonians 5:23-24 says, "And the very God of peace sanctify you wholly; and I pray God your whole spirit and soul and body be preserved blameless unto the coming of our Lord Jesus Christ. 24. Faithful is he that calleth you, who also will do it."

In Romans 7:18-24, Paul says, "For I know that in me (that is, in my flesh,) dwelleth no good thing: for to will is present with me; but how to perform that which is good I find not. 19. For the good that I would I do not: but the evil which I would not, that I do. 20. Now if I do that I would not, it is no more I that do it, but sin that dwelleth in me. 21. I find then a law, that, when I would do good, evil is present with me. 22. For I delight in the law of God after the inward man: 23. But I see another law in my members, warring against the law of my mind, and bringing me into captivity to the law of sin which is in my members. 24. O wretched man that I am! who shall deliver me from the body of this death?"

Paul describes the battle we all face. When I want to do what's right, evil is present with me. I try to serve God, but evil is always nearby. This is not some abstract idea—it's real, and it's serious. We have to take this seriously because souls are on the line. Families are at stake. This is about more than living a life free of regret—it's about saving our families from the evil that constantly tries to encroach upon us. Evil can appear in many forms, and we must abstain from it. But we can't do it alone. Who shall deliver us? Who can save us and preserve us blameless? Only God can do it. He has given us the tools, but we must put them into action. We need to pray constantly that God will help us abstain from all appearance of evil. Don't be intimidated by evil, and don't fear it. It doesn't have power over you—God has given you power over it. I don't want evil in my life, my family, my home, my mind, or my body. Evil is too destructive.

BLAMELESSNESS THROUGH JESUS CHRIST

Keep your head up. Stand in the power of the Lord. Use the weapons He has placed in your hands. If you fail, rise again. You are the temple of the living God, and His Spirit dwells in you. I'm telling you what I've witnessed in my own life—if I do what I know to do and keep His Spirit active in my life, He will do what only He can do. He will put His willpower on top of mine. The life He lived, being tempted yet without sin, will come upon me. When you are tempted, remember that it is written somewhere in the Word of God the answer to overcoming that temptation. Abstain from all appearance of evil.

Rejoice evermore. Pray without ceasing. In everything give thanks, for this is the will of God in Christ Jesus concerning you. Quench not the Spirit. Despise not prophesying. Prove all things; hold fast that which is good. If you do this, with the help of the Holy Spirit, you will abstain from all appearance of evil. The result will be that God will preserve you blameless and sanctify you wholly—body, soul, and spirit. Go forth in victory, in Jesus' name!

CONCLUSION

As we come to the end of this journey through scripture, it's clear that the call to blamelessness is not merely an ideal to be admired from afar, but a daily walk to be pursued with sincerity and faith. Through every chapter, we've explored practical ways to live a life that reflects the character of Christ—rejoicing always, praying without ceasing, giving thanks in all circumstances, proving what is good, holding fast to the Word, and above all, abstaining from the appearance of evil.

Blamelessness, as we've seen, is not perfection achieved by human effort. Rather, it is the state of being preserved by God's grace through faith in Jesus Christ. From the beginning, we learned that none of us are without fault. "For all have sinned and fall short of the glory of God" (Romans 3:23). Yet, we also discovered that God's gift of blamelessness is made possible through the sacrifice of Christ, who forgives our sins and cleanses us from all unrighteousness.

In Chapter 1, we recognized that The Pathway to Blamelessness begins with our surrender to God's sanctifying work in us. Without Jesus as our foundation, we cannot hope to stand before a holy God.

The pursuit of blamelessness starts with embracing His gift of salvation and continues as we walk in faith, empowered by the Holy Spirit.

In Chapter 2, It Is Well, we came face to face with the reality that true happiness and contentment come from knowing that our sins are forgiven, and our future is secured in Christ. Despite trials and challenges, we can rest in the knowledge that God is working all things for our good.

Chapter 3, Sweet Hour of Prayer, taught us the power of communion with God. Prayer is not a duty but a privilege, through which we connect with the Almighty, laying our burdens before Him and receiving His peace in return. It is through prayer that we gain the strength and wisdom to live a life worthy of our calling.

In Chapter 4, we asked the question, Give Thanks, In This? Gratitude is more than a response to good times—it's an act of faith in difficult circumstances. When we choose to give thanks, even in hardship, we acknowledge that God is sovereign and that His plans for us are good.

Chapter 5, Let Go and Let God, was a reminder to release control and trust in God's plan for our lives. So often, our struggles come from trying to manage life on our own terms. But when we surrender fully to His will, we experience the freedom and peace that comes from knowing He is in control.

In Chapter 6, Embrace the Word, we explored the importance of anchoring our lives in scripture. God's Word is not just an instruction manual—it is life itself. Through it, we are equipped, corrected, and encouraged to live in righteousness.

Chapter 7, Prove It! challenged us to test everything and hold fast to that which is good. Discernment is key in our walk with God. We must be able to recognize what aligns with His will and avoid what draws us away from it.

In Chapter 8, Cling to the Good, we were reminded to pursue what is good relentlessly, regardless of the temptations and distractions that surround us. Holding fast to God's goodness ensures that we stay on the path to blamelessness.

Finally, in Chapter 9, we considered the command to Abstain from All Appearance of Evil. As believers, our lives should reflect the holiness of God, both in our actions and in how we present ourselves to the world. By living with discernment and intentionality, we honor God and become a light to those around us.

Now, as we close, we reflect on the charge given to us by the Apostle Paul: "May the God of peace Himself sanctify you completely; and may your whole spirit, soul, and body be preserved blameless at the coming of our Lord Jesus Christ" (1 Thessalonians 5:23). This is the call for every believer—to be sanctified wholly, to be preserved blameless, and to live in the hope of Christ's return.

As you continue your walk with the Lord, remember that blamelessness is not a destination we reach by our strength, but a state of being made possible through the ongoing work of Jesus in our lives. It is a call to be holy as God is holy, and to live each day in full dependence on His grace.

My prayer for you is that you will remain steadfast in your pursuit of blamelessness, trusting that God, who began this good work in you, will be faithful to complete it.

www.ingramcontent.com/pod-product-compliance
Lightning Source LLC
Chambersburg PA
CBHW022110090426
42743CB00008B/786